Songs and Dreams

Introduction

The character of any anthology is determined as much by what is left out as by what is put in.

In this selection I have sought to choose poems which are good in their own right and which will also be stimulating to the minds and imaginations of young people, their teachers and their parents. I make no distinction between 'hard' and 'easy' poems. A child or a student should never be made to feel that a poem is a problem to be sweated and swotted over, but rather is a unique experience to be taken in his stride, just as he takes a new toy, a new picture, and a new song. He may not understand everything, but that does not matter: rational understanding is the least part of poetry appreciation. After all, adults too frequently encounter poems they do not entirely understand. Repeated readings – and this means reading aloud too – will make even fairly difficult poems come alive in the mind, just as constant listening to a new and strange piece of music makes it become familiar and acceptable. As long as even a small degree of contact with the poet's imagination is obtained, one can feel encouraged that young people will find their own ways to a closer understanding of the text.

Some young readers will be able to appreciate and enjoy more than others. After all, there is nothing wrong with not liking poetry or music. But the degree of enjoyment is not as important as the introduction of young minds to a whole new world of colour, sound, movement and ideas. I have tried to include as many modern poets as possible, for the modern child instinctively responds to the modern idiom in verse. It would be an exciting project to publish a poetry anthology for young people composed entirely of contemporary work and including such new elements as pop lyrics, modern folk and rock ballads, concrete poems, protest songs, and work by the very lively new provincial groups in Liverpool, on Tyneside, and in Scotland, Ireland and Wales.

In one respect this anthology is, I think, unique in that it contains translations of Chinese and Japanese poetry, both classical and modern. It is my experience that children and even university students – certainly American students – respond much more quickly and eagerly to the imagery, mood and forms of

Oriental poetry than to those of English verse. They enjoy, too, the making (and the breaking) of mathematical rules in the counting of syllables in Japanese verse forms.

Many of the poems in this anthology are poems whose worth and suitability I have proved in teachers' training courses with my former students at Bath Academy of Arts. They have been used successfully with American children and university students, as well as with the large numbers of Japanese, Chinese, Malay, Swedish, Spanish and French students I have taught.

I should like to thank all those teachers, poets and children who have made suggestions and sent poems. It is impossible to name them all here, but I should like especially to mention Barry Tebb (who kindly made the selection of my own poems which he had found successful in class), Charles Causley, Rena Clayphan, Mona Pehle, Joe Ackerley, Shozo Tokunaga, Rikutaro Fukuda, Tsutomu Fukuda, Michael Bullock, Howard Sergeant, Gloria Evans Davies, Margaret Stanley-Wrench, Charles Higham, Jack Clemo, Robert Morgan, Bryn Griffiths, Haruo Shibuya and John C. Head.

Finally, I should like to express my grateful thanks to Mr and Mrs Charles Rummel of the Japan American Conversation Institute and Keio University in Tokyo for their careful typing.

JAMES KIRKUP

Japan Women's University
Bunkyo-ku
Tokyo
Japan

Contents

9

11

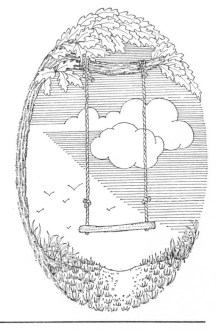

Childhood

Prayer before Birth

I am not yet born; O hear me.
Let not the bloodsucking bat or the rat or the stoat or the
   club-footed ghoul come near me.

I am not yet born; console me.
I fear that the human race may with tall walls wall me,
   with strong drugs dope me, with wise lies lure me,
      on black racks rack me, in blood-baths roll me.

I am not yet born; provide me
With water to dandle me, grass to grow for me, trees to talk
   to me, sky to sing to me, birds and a white light
      in the back of my mind to guide me.

I am not yet born; forgive me
For the sins that in me the world shall commit, my words
   when they speak me, my thoughts when they think me,
      my treason engendered by traitors beyond me,
         my life when they murder by means of my
            hands, my death when they live me.

I am not yet born; rehearse me
In the parts I must play and the cues I must take when
   old men lecture me, bureaucrats hector me, mountains
      frown at me, lovers laugh at me, the white
         waves call me to folly and the desert calls
            me to doom and the beggar refuses
               my gift and my children curse me.

I am not yet born; O hear me.
Let not the man who is beast or who thinks he is God
   come near me.

I am not yet born; O fill me
With strength against those who would freeze my
  humanity, would dragoon me into a lethal automaton,
    would make me a cog in a machine, a thing with
      one face, a thing, and against all those
        who would dissipate my entirety, would
          blow me like thistledown hither and
            thither or hither and thither
              like water held in the
                hands would spill me.

Let them not make me a stone and let them not spill me.
Otherwise kill me.

LOUIS MACNEICE
1907 – 1963

Spring and Fall:
To a Young Child

Márgarét, are you gríeving
Over Goldengrove unleaving?
Leáves, líke the things of man, you
With your fresh thoughts care for, can you?
Áh! ás the heart grows older
It will come to such sights colder
By and by, nor spare a sigh
Though worlds of wanwood leafmeal lie;
And yet you wíll weep and know why.
Now no matter, child, the name:
Sórrow's spríngs áre the same.
Nor mouth had, no nor mind, expressed
What heart heard of, ghost guessed:
It ís the blight man was born for,
It is Margaret you mourn for.

GERARD MANLEY HOPKINS
1844 – 1889

From **The Prelude**

There was a Boy; ye knew him well, ye cliffs
And islands of Winander! – many a time,
At evening, when the earliest stars began
To move along the edges of the hills,
Rising or setting, would he stand alone,
Beneath the trees, or by the glimmering lake;
And there, with fingers interwoven, both hands
Pressed closely palm to palm and to his mouth
Uplifted, he, as through an instrument,
Blew mimic hootings to the silent owls,
That they might answer him. – And they would shout
Across the watery vale, and shout again,
Responsive to his call, – with quivering peals,
And long halloos, and screams, and echoes loud
Redoubled and redoubled; concourse wild
Of jocund din! And when there came a pause
Of silence such as baffled his best skill:
Then, sometimes, in that silence, while he hung
Listening, a gentle shock of mild surprise
Has carried far into his heart the voice
Of mountain-torrents; or the visible scene
Would enter unawares into his mind
With all its solemn imagery, its rocks,
Its woods, and that uncertain heaven received
Into the bosom of the steady lake.

This Boy was taken from his mates, and died
In childhood, ere he was full twelve years old.
Fair are the woods and beauteous is the spot,
The vale where he was born: the church-yard hangs
Upon a slope above the village-school;
And, through that church-yard when my way has led
On summer evenings, I believe that there
A long half-hour together I have stood
Mute – looking at the grave in which he lies!

WILLIAM WORDSWORTH
1770 – 1850

There Was a Child Went Forth

There was a child went forth every day,
And the first object he look'd upon, that object he became,
And that object became part of him for the day or a
    certain part of the day,
Or for many years or stretching cycles of years.

The early lilacs became part of this child,
And grass and white and red morning-glories, and white
    and red clover, and the song of the phoebe-bird,
And the Third-month lambs and the sow's pink-faint litter,
    and the mare's foal and the cow's calf,
And the noisy brood of the barnyard or by the mire of the
    pond-side,
And the fish suspending themselves so curiously below
    there, and the beautiful curious liquid,
And the water-plants with their graceful flat heads, all
    became part of him.

The field-sprouts of Fourth-month and Fifth-month
    became part of him,
Winter-grain sprouts and those of the light-yellow corn,
    and the esculent roots of the garden,
And the apple-trees cover'd with blossoms and the fruit
    afterward, and wood-berries, and the commonest
    weeds by the road,
And the old drunkard staggering home from the outhouse
    of the tavern whence he had lately risen,
And the schoolmistress that pass'd on her way to the school,
And the friendly boys that pass'd, and the quarrelsome
    boys,
And the tidy and fresh-cheek'd girls, and the barefoot
    negro boy and girl,
And all the changes of city and country wherever he went.

His own parents, he that had father'd him and she that had
    conceiv'd him in her womb and birth'd him,
They gave this child more of themselves than that,
They gave him afterward every day, they became part of
    him.

The mother at home quietly placing the dishes on the
supper-table,
The mother with mild words, clean her cap and gown, a
wholesome odor falling off her person and clothes as
she walks by,
The father, strong, self-sufficient, manly, mean, anger'd,
unjust,
The blow, the quick loud word, the tight bargain, the
crafty lure,
The family usages, the language, the company, the furniture, the yearning and swelling heart,
Affection that will not be gainsay'd, the sense of what is
real, the thought if after all it should prove unreal,
The doubts of day-time and the doubts of night-time, the
curious whether and how,
Whether that which appears so is so, or is it all flashes and
specks?
Men and women crowding fast in the streets, if they are
not flashes and specks what are they?
The streets themselves and the façades of houses, and goods
in the windows,
Vehicles, teams, the heavy-plank'd wharves, the huge crossing at the ferries,
The village on the highland seen from afar at sunset, the
river between,
Shadows, aureola and mist, the light falling on roofs and
gables of white or brown two miles off,
The schooner near by sleepily dropping down the tide, the
little boat slack-tow'd astern,
The hurrying tumbling waves, quick-broken crests, slap-
ping,
The strata of color'd clouds, the long bar of maroon-tint
away solitary by itself, the spread of purity it lies
motionless in,
The horizon's edge, the flying sea-crow, the fragrance of
salt marsh and shore mud,
These became part of that child who went forth every day,
and who now goes, and will always go forth every
day.

WALT WHITMAN
1819 – 1892

A Map of the Western Part of the
County of Essex in England

Something forgotten for twenty years: though my fathers
and mothers came from Cordova and Vitepsk and
  Caernarvon,
and though I am a citizen of the United States and less a
stranger here than anywhere else, perhaps,
I am Essex-born:
Cranbrook Wash called me into its dark tunnel,
the little streams of Valentines heard my resolves,
Roding held my head above water when I thought it was
drowning me; in Hainault only a haze of thin trees
stood between the red doubledecker buses and
  the boar-hunt,
the spirit of merciful Philippa glimmered there.
Pergo Park knew me, and Clavering, and
  Havering-atte-Bower,
Stanford Rivers lost me in osier-beds, Stapleford Abbots
sent me safe home on the dark road after
  Simeon-quiet evensong,
Wanstead drew me over and over into its basic poetry,
in its serpentine lake I saw bass-viols among the golden
  dead leaves,
through its trees the ghost of a great house.
In Ilford High Road I saw the multitudes passing pale
  under the
light of flaring sundown, seven kings
in sombre starry robes gathered at Seven Kings
the place of law
where my birth and marriage are recorded
and the death of my father. Woodford Wells
where an old house was named The Naked Beauty (a white
statue forlorn in its garden)
saw the meeting and parting of two sisters
(forgotten? and further away
the hill before Thaxted? where peace befell us? not once
but many times?)
All the Ivans dreaming of their villages
all the Marias dreaming of their walled cities,
picking up fragments of New World slowly
not knowing how to put them together nor how to join
image with image, now I know how it was with you,
  an old map

made long before I was born shows ancient
rights of way where I walked when I was ten
        burning with desire
for the world's great splendours, a child who traced voyages
indelibly all over the atlas, who now in a far country
remembers the first river, the first
field, bricks, and lumber dumped in it ready for building,
that new smell, and remembers
the walls of the garden, the first light.

DENISE LEVERTOV
born 1923

Message from Home

Do you remember, when you were first a child,
Nothing in the world seemed strange to you?
You perceived, for the first time, shapes already familiar,
And seeing, you knew that you have always known
The lichen on the rock, fern-leaves, the flowers of thyme,
As if the elements newly met in your body
Caught up into the momentary vortex of your living
Still kept the knowledge of a former state,
In you retained recollection of cloud and ocean,
The branching tree, the dancing flame.

Now when nature's darkness seems strange to you,
And you walk, an alien, in the streets of cities,
Remember earth breathed you into her with the air, with the
        sun's rays,
Laid you in her waters asleep, to dream
With the brown trout among the milfoil roots,
From substance of star and ocean fashioned you,
At the same source conceived you
As sun and foliage, fish and stream.

KATHLEEN RAINE
born 1908

Trebetherick

We used to picnic where the thrift
   Grew deep and tufted to the edge;
We saw the yellow foam-flakes drift
   In trembling sponges on the ledge
Below us, till the wind would lift
   Them up the cliff and o'er the hedge.
Sand in the sandwiches, wasps in the tea,
Sun on our bathing-dresses heavy with the wet,
Squelch of the bladder-wrack waiting for the sea,
Fleas round the tamarisk, an early cigarette.

From where the coastguard houses stood
   One used to see, below the hill,
The lichened branches of a wood
   In summer silver-cool and still;
And there the Shade of Evil could
   Stretch out at us from Shilla Mill.
Thick with sloe and blackberry, uneven in the light,
Lonely ran the hedge, the heavy meadow was remote,
The oldest part of Cornwall was the wood as black as night,
And the pheasant and the rabbit lay torn open at the throat.

But when a storm was at its height,
   And feathery slate was black in rain,
And tamarisks were hung with light
   And golden sand was brown again,
Spring tide and blizzard would unite
   And sea came flooding up the lane.
Waves full of treasure then were roaring up the beach,
Ropes round our mackintoshes, waders warm and dry,
We waited for the wreckage to come swirling into reach,
Ralph, Vasey, Alastair, Biddy, John and I.

Then roller into roller curled
   And thundered down the rocky bay,
And we were in a water-world
   Of rain and blizzard, sea and spray,
And one against the other hurled
   We struggled round to Greenaway.
Blesséd be St Enodoc, blessed be the wave,
Blesséd be the springy turf, we pray, pray to thee,
Ask for our children all the happy days you gave
To Ralph, Vasey, Alastair, Biddy, John and me.

JOHN BETJEMAN
born 1906

The Rainbow

My heart leaps up when I behold
   A rainbow in the sky:
So was it when my life began;
So is it now I am a man;
So be it when I shall grow old,
   Or let me die!
The Child is father of the Man;
And I could wish my days to be
Bound each to each by natural piety.

WILLIAM WORDSWORTH
1770 – 1850

American Names

I have fallen in love with American names,
The sharp names that never get fat,
The snakeskin-titles of mining-claims,
The plumed war-bonnet of Medicine Hat,
Tucson and Deadwood and Lost Mule Flat.

Seine and Piave are silver spoons,
But the spoonbowl-metal is thin and worn,
There are English counties like hunting-tunes
Played on the keys of a postboy's horn,
But I will remember where I was born.

I will remember Carquinez Straits,
Little French Lick and Lundy's Lane,
The Yankee ships and the Yankee dates
And the bullet-towns of Calamity Jane.
I will remember Skunktown Plain.

I will fall in love with a Salem tree
And a rawhide quirt from Santa Cruz,
I will get me a bottle of Boston sea
And a blue-gum nigger to sing me blues.
I am tired of loving a foreign muse.

Rue des Martyrs and Bleeding-Heart-Yard,
Senlis, Pisa, and Blindman's Oast,
It is a magic ghost you guard
But I am sick for a newer ghost,
Harrisburg, Spartanburg, Painted Post.

Henry and John were never so
And Henry and John were always right?
Granted, but when it was time to go
And the tea and the laurels had stood all night,
Did they never watch for Nantucket Light?

I shall not rest quiet in Montparnasse.
I shall not lie easy at Winchelsea.
You may bury my body in Sussex grass,
You may bury my tongue at Champmédy.
I shall not be there.   I shall rise and pass.
Bury my heart at Wounded Knee.

STEPHEN VINCENT BENÉT
1898 – 1943

The Cwm above Penrhiwceiber

There was sparkling water, too small
For a river, too big for a stream.
As boys we sampled it as early
As April when the weather changed.
We dammed it and dived off a tree
And gasped in the trout-cold water.
We crept through dark growth
Of young and old trees, tall
Fern and tangled bramble where the sun
Could only get fingers through.
The ground sagged under foot
And bird and insect silence
Was rich with arrows of history.
Ghosts sighed in a trapped
Breeze and every indigo shadow
Hid a skeleton and a sword.
Out in the sunlight we shouted
Our fears away and romped home,
Glancing back at the tremulous
Waves of trees in our cwm
Now buried under rubbish from pits.

ROBERT MORGAN
born 1921

Warning to Children

Children, if you dare to think
Of the greatness, rareness, muchness,
Fewness of this precious only
Endless world in which you say
You live, you think of things like this:
Blocks of slate enclosing dappled
Red and green, enclosing tawny
Yellow nets, enclosing white
And black acres of dominoes,
Where a neat brown paper parcel
Tempts you to untie the string.
In the parcel a small island,
On the island a large tree,
On the tree a husky fruit.
Strip the husk and pare the rind off:
In the kernel you will see
Blocks of slate enclosed by dappled
Red and green, enclosed by tawny
Yellow nets, enclosed by white
And black acres of dominoes,
Where the same brown paper parcel –
Children, leave the string alone!
For who dares undo the parcel
Finds himself at once inside it,
On the island, in the fruit,
Blocks of slate about his head,
Finds himself enclosed by dappled
Green and red, enclosed by yellow
Tawny nets, enclosed by black
And white acres of dominoes,
With the same brown paper parcel
Still unopened on his knee.
And, if he then should dare to think
Of the fewness, muchness, rareness,
Greatness of this endless only
Precious world in which he says
He lives – he then unties the string.

ROBERT GRAVES
born 1895

Fern Hill

Now as I was young and easy under the apple boughs
About the lilting house and happy as the grass was green,
   The night above the dingle starry,
     Time let me hail and climb
   Golden in the heydays of his eyes,
And honoured among the wagons I was prince of the apple towns
And once below a time I lordly had the trees and leaves
     Trail with daisies and barley
   Down the rivers of the windfall light.

And as I was green and carefree, famous among the barns
About the happy yard and singing as the farm was home,
   In the sun that is young once only
     Time let me play and be
   Golden in the mercy of his means,
And green and golden I was huntsman and herdsman, the calves
Sang to my horn, the foxes on the hills barked clear and cold,
     And the sabbath rang slowly
   In the pebbles of the holy streams.

All the sun long it was running, it was lovely, the hay
Fields high as the house, the tunes from the chimneys, it was air
   And playing, lovely and watery
     And fire green as grass.
   And nightly under the simple stars
As I rode to sleep the owls were bearing the farm away,
All the moon long I heard, blessed among stables, the nightjars
     Flying with the ricks, and the horses
      Flashing into the dark.

And then to awake, and the farm, like a wanderer white
With the dew, come back, the cock on his shoulder: it was all
   Shining, it was Adam and maiden,
     The sky gathered again
   And the sun grew round that very day.

So it must have been after the birth of the simple light
In the first, spinning place, the spellbound horses walking warm
   Out of the whinnying green stable
      On to the fields of praise.

And honoured among foxes and pheasants by the gay house
Under the new made clouds and happy as the heart was long,
   In the sun born over and over,
      I ran my heedless ways,
   My wishes raced through the house high hay
And nothing I cared, at my sky blue trades, that time allows
In all his tuneful turning so few and such morning songs
   Before the children green and golden
      Follow him out of grace,

Nothing I cared, in the lamb white days, that time would take me
Up to the swallow thronged loft by the shadow of my hand,
   In the moon that is always rising,
      Nor that riding to sleep
   I should hear him fly with the high fields
And wake to the farm forever fled from the childless land.
Oh as I was young and easy in the mercy of his means,
      Time held me green and dying
     Though I sang in my chains like the sea.

DYLAN THOMAS
1914 – 1953

I Remember, I Remember

I remember, I remember,
The house where I was born,
The little window where the sun
Came peeping in at morn;
He never came a wink too soon,
Nor brought too long a day,
But now, I often wish the night
Had borne my breath away!

I remember, I remember,
The roses, red and white,
The vi'lets, and the lily-cups,
Those flowers made of light!
The lilacs where the robin built,
And where my brother set
The laburnum on his birthday, –
The tree is living yet!

I remember, I remember,
Where I was used to swing,
And thought the air must rush as fresh
To swallows on the wing;
My spirit flew in feathers then,
That is so heavy now,
And summer pools could hardly cool
The fever on my brow!

I remember, I remember,
The fir trees dark and high;
I used to think their slender tops
Were close against the sky:
It was a childish ignorance,
But now 'tis little joy
To know I'm farther off from heav'n
Than when I was a boy.

THOMAS HOOD
1799 – 1845

The Retreat

Happy those early days, when I
Shin'd in my Angel-infancy!
Before I understood this place
Appointed for my second race,
Or taught my soul to fancy aught
But a white celestial thought:
When yet I had not walk'd above
A mile or two from my first Love,
And looking back – at that short space –
Could see a glimpse of His bright face:
When on some gilded cloud, or flow'r,
My gazing soul would dwell an hour,
And in those weaker glories spy
Some shadows of eternity:
Before I taught my tongue to wound
My Conscience with a sinful sound,
Or had the black art to dispense
A several sin to ev'ry sense,
But felt through all this fleshly dress
Bright *shoots* of everlastingness.

O how I long to travel back,
And tread again that ancient track!
That I might once more reach that plain
Where first I left my glorious train;
From whence th' enlightened spirit sees
That shady City of Palm-trees.
But ah! my soul with too much stay
Is drunk, and staggers in the way!
Some men a forward motion love,
But I by backward steps would move;
And when this dust falls to the urn,
In that state I came, return.

HENRY VAUGHAN
1622 – 1695

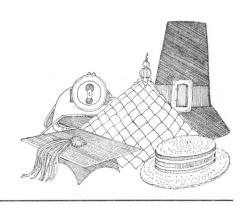

Some people

Guy Fawkes' Day

I am the caught, the cooked, the candled man
With flames for fingers and whose thin eyes fountain,
I send on the stiff air my shooting stare
And at my shoulder bear the burning mountain.

I open on the dark my wound of speeches,
With stabs, with stars its seven last words wear,
My tongue of torches with the salamander
Breeds conversaziones of despair.

Milled in the minted light my skin of silver
Now curls, now kindles on the thicket's bone,
And fired with flesh in sepulchres of slumber
Walks the white night with sparks and showers sown.

At my fixed feet soldiers my coat of carbon
Slit with the speared sky. Their sacked eyes scan
My mask of medals. In bright mirrors of breath
Our faces fuse in death. My name is man.

CHARLES CAUSLEY
born 1917

C

A Butcher

Whoe'er has gone thro' London Street,
Has seen a Butcher gazing at his
      meat
  And how he keeps
  Gloating upon a sheep's
Or bullock's personals, as if his own;
  How he admires his halves
  And quarters – and his calves,
As if in truth upon his own legs grown; –
  His fat! his suet!
His kidneys peeping elegantly thro' it!
  His thick flank!
  And his thin!
     His shank!
     His shin!
Skin of his skin, and bone too of his
      bone!

    With what an air
He stands aloof, across the thorough-
      fare
Gazing – and will not let a body by,
Tho' buy! buy! buy! be constantly
     his cry.
Meanwhile with arms a-kimbo, and
     a pair
Of Rhodian legs he revels in a stare
At his Joint Stock – for one may call
     it so,
  Howbeit, without a Co.
The dotage of self-love was never
     fonder
Than he of his brute bodies all a-row;
Narcissus in the wave did never ponder
  With love so strong,
  On his 'portrait charmant'
As our vain Butcher on his carcase
     yonder.

Look at his sleek round skull!
How bright his cheek, how rubicund
        his nose is!
His visage seems to be
    Ripe for beef-tea;
Of brutal juices the whole man is
        full. –
In fact, fulfilling the metempsychosis,
The Butcher is already half a Bull.

THOMAS HOOD
1799 – 1845

Low Seam Miner

And he returns day after day
To crouch on knees and side
In a seam two feet high
With a patch of cold light
Making a hole in darkness
Where the roof bends bleeding posts
Above his tilted head.
His tense hands curled on a shaft
Stab in slow arcs over the coal.
He works . . . and listens to the roof and floor
Straining to close the gap where he lies.
Yet he returns day after day
Eager and unafraid to his bleak cell.

ROBERT MORGAN
born 1921

The Collier

When I was born on Amman hill
A dark bird crossed the sun.
Sharp on the floor the shadow fell;
I was the youngest son.

And when I went to the County School
I worked in a shaft of light.
In the wood of the desk I cut my name:
Dai for Dynamite.

The tall black hills my brothers stood;
Their lessons all were done.
From the door of the school when I ran out
They frowned to watch me run.

The slow grey bells they rung a chime
Surly with grief or age.
Clever or clumsy, lad or lout,
All would look for a wage.

I learnt the valley flowers' names
And the rough bark knew my knees.
I brought home trout from the river
And spotted eggs from the trees.

A coloured coat I was given to wear
Where the lights of the rough land shone.
Still jealous of my favour
The tall black hills looked on.

They dipped my coat in the blood of a kid
And they cast me down a pit,
And although I crossed with strangers
There was no way up from it.

Soon as I went from the County School
I worked in a shaft. Said Jim,
'You will get your chain of gold, my lad,
But not for a likely time.'

And one said, 'Jack was not raised up
When the wind blew out the light
Though he interpreted their dreams
And guessed their fears by night.'

And Tom, he shivered his leper's lamp
For the stain that round him grew;
And I heard mouths pray in the after-damp
When the picks would not break through.

They changed words there in darkness
And still through my head they run,
And white on my limbs is the linen sheet
And gold on my neck the sun.

VERNON WATKINS
1906 – 1967

The Sage and His Onions

I am the great Professor Jowett:
What there is to know, I know it.
I am the Master of Balliol College,
And what I don't know isn't knowledge.

ANON.

The River-Merchant's Wife: A Letter

While my hair was still cut straight across my forehead
I played about the front gate, pulling flowers.
You came by on bamboo stilts, playing horse,
You walked about my seat, playing with blue plums.
And we went on living in the village of Chokan:
Two small people, without dislike or suspicion.

At fourteen I married My Lord you.
I never laughed, being bashful.
Lowering my head, I looked at the wall.
Called to, a thousand times, I never looked back.

At fifteen I stopped scowling,
I desired my dust to be mingled with yours
Forever and forever and forever.
Why should I climb the look out?

At sixteen you departed.
You went into far Ku-to-yen, by the river of swirling eddies,
And you have been gone five months.
The monkeys make sorrowful noise overhead.

You dragged your feet when you went out.
By the gate now, the moss is grown, the different mosses,
Too deep to clear them away!
The leaves fall early this autumn, in wind.
The paired butterflies are already yellow with August
Over the grass in the West garden;
They hurt me. I grow older.
If you are coming down through the narrows of the river Kiang,
Please let me know beforehand,
And I will come out to meet you
                         As far as Cho-fu-Sa.

RIHAKU
8th Century A.D.

*Translated from the Chinese
by Ezra Pound*

The Solitary Reaper

Behold her, single in the field,
  Yon solitary Highland Lass!
Reaping and singing by herself;
  Stop here, or gently pass!
Alone she cuts and binds the grain,
And sings a melancholy strain;
O listen! for the Vale profound
Is overflowing with the sound.

No Nightingale did ever chaunt
  More welcome notes to weary bands
Of travellers in some shady haunt,
  Among Arabian sands:
A voice so thrilling ne'er was heard
In spring-time from the Cuckoo-bird,
Breaking the silence of the seas
Among the farthest Hebrides.

Will no one tell me what she sings? –
  Perhaps the plaintive numbers flow
For old, unhappy, far-off things,
  And battles long ago:
Or is it some more humble lay,
Familiar matter of to-day?
Some natural sorrow, loss, or pain,
That has been, and may be again?

Whate'er the theme, the Maiden sang
  As if her song could have no ending;
I saw her singing at her work,
  And o'er the sickle bending; –
I listen'd, motionless and still;
And, as I mounted up the hill,
The music in my heart I bore,
Long after it was heard no more.

WILLIAM WORDSWORTH
1770 – 1850

Gipsies

The gipsies seek wide sheltering woods again,
With droves of horses flock to mark their lane,
And trample on dead leaves, and hear the sound,
And look and see the black clouds gather round,
And set their camps, and free from muck and mire,
And gather stolen sticks to make the fire.
The roasted hedgehog, bitter though as gall,
Is eaten up and relished by them all.
They know the woods and every fox's den
And get their living far away from men;
The shooters ask them where to find the game,
The rabbits know them and are almost tame.
The aged women, tawny with the smoke,
Go with the winds and crack the rotted oak.

JOHN CLARE
1793 – 1864

The Ricksha Puller

The wind roars and rocks treetops;
On the tip of his nose raindrops gather in a growing trickle.
A pitiful, small lamp on his ricksha
Cannot dispel the dark shadows around.

A strange puzzle is his thought.
Unmindful of the raging storm,
He sits still, like a drenched hen,
The night is growing old; what is he waiting for?

TSANG K'O-CHIA
born c. 1910
Translated from the Chinese
by Kai-Yu Hsu

The Blind Boy

O say! what is that Thing call'd Light,
　Which I must ne'er enjoy;
What is the Blessing of the Sight,
　O tell your poor Blind Boy!

You talk of wond'rous Things you see,
　You say the Sun shines bright;
I feel him warm, but how can he
　Or make it Day or Night?

My Day or Night myself I make,
　Whene'er I sleep or play,
And cou'd I ever keep awake,
　It wou'd be always Day.

With heavy Sighs, I often hear,
　You mourn my hapless Woe;
But sure, with Patience I can bear
　A Loss I ne'er can know.

Then let not what I cannot have
　My Chear of Mind destroy;
Whilst thus I sing, I am a King,
　Altho' a poor Blind Boy.

COLLEY CIBBER
1671 – 1757

The Lonely Scarecrow

My poor old bones – I've only two –
A broomshank and a broken stave,
My ragged gloves are a disgrace,
My one peg-foot is in the grave.

I wear the labourer's old clothes;
Coat, shirt and trousers all undone.
I bear my cross upon a hill
In rain and shine, in snow and sun.

I cannot help the way I look.
My funny hat is full of hay.
– O, wild birds, come and nest in me!
Why do you always fly away?

JAMES KIRKUP
born 1923

One Girl

Like the sweet apple which reddens upon
    the topmost bough,
Atop on the topmost twig, – which the
    pluckers forgot, somehow, –
Forgot it not, nay, but got it not, for none
    could get it till now.

Like the wild hyacinth flower which on the
    hills is found,
Which the passing feet of the shepherds
    for ever tear and wound,
Until the purple blossom is trodden in the
    ground.

SAPPHO
c. 610 B.C.
Translated from the Greek
by Dante Gabriel Rossetti

The Sluggard

'Tis the Voice of the Sluggard; I heard him complain,
'You have wak'd me too soon, I must slumber again.'
As the Door on its Hinges, so he on his Bed,
Turns his Sides and his Shoulders and his heavy Head.

'A little more Sleep, and a little more Slumber;'
Thus he wastes half his Days and his Hours without Number;
And when he gets up, he sits folding his Hands,
Or walks about saunt'ring, or trifling he stands.

I pass'd by his Garden, and saw the wild Brier,
The Thorn and the Thistle grow broader and higher;
The Clothes that hang on him are turning to Rags;
And his Money still wastes, till he starves or he begs.

I made him a Visit, still hoping to find
He had took better Care for improving his Mind:
He told me his Dreams, talk'd of Eating and Drinking;
But he scarce reads his Bible, and never loves Thinking.

Said I then to my Heart, 'Here's a Lesson for me;'
That Man's but a Picture of what I might be:
But thanks to my Friends for their Care in my Breeding,
Who taught me betimes to love Working and Reading.

ISAAC WATTS
1674–1748

Richard Cory

Whenever Richard Cory went down town,
We people on the pavement looked at him:
He was a gentleman from sole to crown,
Clean favored, and imperially slim.

And he was always quietly arrayed,
And he was always human when he talked;
But still he fluttered pulses when he said,
'Good morning,' and he glittered when he walked.

And he was rich – yes, richer than a king –
And admirably schooled in every grace:
In fine, we thought that he was everything
To make us wish that we were in his place.

So on we worked, and waited for the light,
And went without the meat, and cursed the bread;
And Richard Cory, one calm summer night,
Went home and put a bullet through his head.

EDWIN ARLINGTON ROBINSON
1869 – 1935

The Lady who Offers Her Looking-Glass to Venus

Venus, take my Votive Glass:
Since I am not what I was,
What from this Day I shall be,
Venus, let Me never see.

MATTHEW PRIOR
1664 – 1721

Cities and machines

Pastoral

When I was younger
it was plain to me
I must make something of myself.
Older now
I walk back streets
admiring the houses
of the very poor:
roof out of line with sides
the yards cluttered
with old chicken wire, ashes,
furniture gone wrong;
the fences and outhouses
built of barrel-staves
and parts of boxes, all,
if I am fortunate,
smeared a bluish green
that properly weathered
pleases me best
of all colors.
                        No one
will believe this
of vast import to the nation.

WILLIAM CARLOS WILLIAMS
1883 – 1963

A Description of Greenock
Ballad in Blank Verse of the
Making of a Poet

. . . this grey town
That pipes the morning up before the lark
With shrieking steam, and from a hundred stalks
Lacquers the sooty sky; where hammers clang
On iron hulls, and cranes in harbours creak
Rattle and swing, whole cargoes on their necks;
Where men sweat gold that others hoard or spend,
And lurk like vermin in their narrow streets . . .

JOHN DAVIDSON
1857 – 1909

I Like to See it Lap the Miles

I like to see it lap the miles,
And lick the valleys up,
And stop to feed itself at tanks;
And then, prodigious, step

Around a pile of mountains,
And, supercilious, peer
In shanties by the sides of roads;
And then a quarry pare

To fit its sides, and crawl between,
Complaining all the while
In horrid, hooting stanza;
Then chase itself down hill

And neigh like Boanerges;
Then, punctual as a star,
Stop – docile and omnipotent –
At its own stable door.

EMILY DICKINSON
1830–1886

The Silver Mine

Stark naked, the men
Stand together in clusters;
Swinging great hammers
They smash into fragments
The lumps of unwrought metal.

TACHIBANA AKEMI
1812 – 1868
*Translated from the Japanese
by Donald Keene*

48

The Dark City

The lighted city is dark, but somewhere a bus
Glows and flares up in a hearth of coal-black space
And with its headlights singles out a face
Lost in a night of enormous loneliness.

Lost in the night of enormous loneliness
Which is his life, man looks for signs of light:
They are the small camp fires which put to flight
The beasts that prowl towards his helplessness.

The beasts that prowl towards our helplessness
Are brave in darkness, but in light they run
To deep subconscious caves in the mind of man
For whom a light is a home in homelessness.

CLIFFORD DYMENT
born 1914

Upon Westminster Bridge

Earth has not anything to show more fair:
Dull would he be of soul who could pass by
A sight so touching in its majesty:
This City now doth like a garment wear
The beauty of the morning; silent, bare,
Ships, towers, domes, theatres, and temples lie
Open unto the fields, and to the sky;
All bright and glittering in the smokeless air.
Never did sun more beautifully steep
In his first splendour valley, rock or hill;
Ne'er saw I, never felt, a calm so deep!
The river glideth at his own sweet will:
Dear God! the very houses seem asleep;
And all that mighty heart is lying still!

WILLIAM WORDSWORTH
1770 – 1850

Night Mail

This is the Night Mail crossing the Border,
Bringing the cheque and the postal order,

Letters for the rich, letters for the poor,
The shop at the corner, the girl next door.

Pulling up Beattock, a steady climb:
The gradient's against her, but she's on time.

Past cotton-grass and moorland boulder,
Shovelling white steam over her shoulder,

Snorting noisily, she passes
Silent miles of wind-bent grasses.

Birds turn their heads as she approaches,
Stare from bushes at her blank-faced coaches.

Sheep-dogs cannot turn her course;
They slumber on with paws across.

In the farm she passes no one wakes,
But a jug in a bedroom gently shakes.

Dawn freshens. Her climb is done.
Down towards Glasgow she descends,
Towards the steam tugs yelping down a glade of cranes,
Towards the fields of apparatus, the furnaces
Set on the dark plain like gigantic chessmen.
All Scotland waits for her:
In dark glens, beside pale-green lochs,
Men long for news.

Letters of thanks, letters from banks,
Letters of joy from girl and boy,
Receipted bills and invitations
To inspect new stock or to visit relations,
And applications for situations,
And timid lovers' declarations,
And gossip, gossip from all the nations,
News circumstantial, news financial,
Letters with holiday snaps to enlarge in,
Letters with faces scrawled on the margin,
Letters from uncles, cousins and aunts,
Letters to Scotland from the South of France,
Letters of condolence to Highlands and Lowlands,
Written on paper of every hue,
The pink, the violet, the white and the blue,
The chatty, the catty, the boring, the adoring,
The cold and official and the heart's outpouring,
Clever, stupid, short and long,
The typed and the printed and the spelt all wrong.

Thousands are still asleep,
Dreaming of terrifying monsters
Or a friendly tea beside the band in Cranston's or Crawford's:
Asleep in working Glasgow, asleep in well-set Edinburgh,
Asleep in granite Aberdeen,
They continue their dreams,
But shall wake soon and hope for letters,
And none will hear the postman's knock
Without a quickening of the heart.
For who can bear to feel himself forgotten?

W. H. AUDEN
born 1907

she being Brand

she being Brand
-new ;and you
know consequently a
little stiff i was
careful of her and(having

thoroughly oiled the universal
joint tested my gas felt of
her radiator made sure her springs were O.

K.)i went right to it flooded-the-carburetor cranked her

up, slipped the
clutch(and then somehow got into reverse she
kicked what
the hell)next
minute i was back in neutral tried and

again slo-wly ;bare,ly nudg. ing(my

lev-er Right –
oh and her gears being in
A 1 shape passed
from low through
second-in-to-high like
greased lightning just as we turned the corner of Divinity

avenue i touched the accelerator and give

her the juice,good
was the first ride and believe i we was
happy to see how nice she acted right up to
the last minute coming back down by the Public
Gardens i slammed on
the

internalexpanding
&
externalcontracting
brakes Bothatonce and

brought allofher tremB
-ling
to a :dead.

stand-
;Still)

E. E. CUMMINGS
1894 – 1962

The Subway in New York

Here forests of skyscrapers
Compete with one another in height
Among the splendour and grandeur
Which this mammoth city prides in.
I found, however, its subway quite miserable.
The window-frames of the car I got into
Were encrusted with much rust.
Its matted seats were worn
And torn and disembowelled.
Dirty were the window-panes,
Spoiled with many rain-marks,
Through which I could see only dimly
The shifting scenes of the outside world,
When the car came out of the long, noisy tube.
Quite disappointed, I stole a glance
At the magazine a girl was reading
And found she was poring over
The recent fashions in Paris.

TSUTOMU FUKUDA
born 1905

From **Don Juan**

This is the patent age of new inventions
    For killing bodies, and for saving souls,
All propagated with the best intentions;
    Sir Humphry Davy's lantern, by which coals
Are safely mined for in the mode he mentions,
    Tomboctoo travels, voyages to the Poles,
Are ways to benefit mankind, as true,
Perhaps, as shooting them at Waterloo.

GEORGE GORDON, LORD BYRON
1788 – 1824

The Reverie of Poor Susan

At the corner of Wood Street, when daylight appears,
Hangs a Thrush that sings loud, it has sung for three years:
Poor Susan has passed by the spot, and has heard
In the silence of morning the song of the Bird.

'Tis a note of enchantment; what ails her? She sees
A mountain ascending, a vision of trees;
Bright volumes of vapour through Lothbury glide,
And a river flows on through the vale of Cheapside.

Green pastures she views in the midst of the dale,
Down which she so often has tripped with her pail;
And a single small cottage, a nest like a dove's,
The one only dwelling on earth that she loves.

She looks, and her heart is in heaven: but they fade,
The mist and the river, the hill and the shade:
The stream will not flow, and the hill will not rise,
And the colours have all passed away from her eyes!

WILLIAM WORDSWORTH
1770 – 1850

Limited

I am riding on a limited express, one of the crack trains
    of the nation.
Hurtling across the prairie into blue haze and dark air
    go fifteen all-steel coaches holding a thousand
    people.
(All the coaches shall be scrap and rust and all the men
    and women laughing in the diners and sleepers
    shall pass to ashes.)
I ask a man in the smoker where he is going and he
    answers: 'Omaha.'

CARL SANDBURG
1878 – 1967

War and peace

Overnight in the Apartment by the River

While the evening here is approaching the mountain paths,
I come to this high up chamber, very close to the Water-Gate.
Thin clouds rest on the edge of cliffs;
A lonely moon turns among the waves.

A line of cranes in flight is silent;
A pack of wolves baying over their prey breaks the quiet.
I cannot sleep because I am concerned about wars,
Because I am powerless to amend the world.

TU FU
A.D. 712 – 770

*Translated from the Chinese
by William Hung*

An Irish Airman Foresees His Death

I know that I shall meet my fate
Somewhere among the clouds above;
Those that I fight I do not hate,
Those that I guard I do not love;
My country is Kiltartan Cross,
My countrymen Kiltartan's poor,
No likely end could bring them loss
Or leave them happier than before.
Nor law, nor duty bade me fight,
Nor public men, nor cheering crowds,
A lonely impulse of delight
Drove to this tumult in the clouds;
I balanced all, brought all to mind,
The years to come seemed waste of breath,
A waste of breath the years behind
In balance with this life, this death.

WILLIAM BUTLER YEATS
1865 – 1939

Hohenlinden

On Linden, when the sun was low,
All bloodless lay the untrodden snow,
And dark as winter was the flow
   Of Iser, rolling rapidly.

But Linden saw another sight,
When the drum beat at dead of night
Commanding fires of death to light
   The darkness of her scenery.

By torch and trumpet fast arrayed,
Each horseman drew his battle blade,
And furious every charger neighed
   To join the dreadful revelry.

Then shook the hills with thunder riven;
Then rushed the steed to battle driven;
And louder than the bolts of heaven
   Far flashed the red artillery.

But redder yet that light shall glow
On Linden's hills of stainèd snow;
And bloodier yet the torrent flow
   Of Iser, rolling rapidly.

'Tis morn, but scarce yon level sun
Can pierce the war-clouds, rolling dun,
Where furious Frank and fiery Hun
   Shout in their sulphurous canopy.

The combat deepens. On, ye Brave,
Who rush to glory, or the grave!
Wave, Munich! all thy banners wave,
   And charge with all thy chivalry!

Few, few shall part, where many meet!
The snow shall be their winding-sheet,
And every turf beneath their feet
    Shall be a soldier's sepulchre.

THOMAS CAMPBELL
1777 – 1844

The Man He Killed

'Had he and I but met
    By some old ancient inn,
We should have sat us down to wet
    Right many a nipperkin!

'But ranged as infantry,
    And staring face to face,
I shot at him as he at me,
    And killed him in his place.

'I shot him dead because –
    Because he was my foe,
Just so: my foe of course he was;
    That's clear enough; although

'He thought he'd 'list, perhaps,
    Off-hand like – just as I;
Was out of work, had sold his traps –
    No other reason why.

'Yes; quaint and curious war is!
    You shoot a fellow down
You'd treat if met where any bar is,
    Or help to half-a-crown.'

THOMAS HARDY
1840 – 1928

Strange Meeting

It seemed that out of battle I escaped
Down some profound dull tunnel, long since scooped
Through granites which titanic wars had groined.
Yet also there encumbered sleepers groaned,
Too fast in thought or death to be bestirred.
Then, as I probed them, one sprang up, and stared
With piteous recognition in fixed eyes,
Lifting distressful hands as if to bless.
And by his smile, I knew that sullen hall,
By his dead smile I knew we stood in Hell.
With a thousand pains that vision's face was grained;
Yet no blood reached there from the upper ground,
And no guns thumped, or down the flues made moan.
'Strange friend,' I said, 'here is no cause to mourn.'
'None,' said the other, 'save the undone years,
The hopelessness. Whatever hope is yours,
Was my life also; I went hunting wild
After the wildest beauty in the world,
Which lies not calm in eyes, or braided hair,
But mocks the steady running of the hour,
And if it grieves, grieves richlier than here.
For by my glee might many men have laughed,
And of my weeping something had been left,
Which must die now. I mean the truth untold,
The pity of war, the pity war distilled.
Now men will go content with what we spoiled,
Or, discontent, boil bloody, and be spilled.
They will be swift with swiftness of the tigress.
None will break ranks, though nations trek from progress.
Courage was mine, and I had mystery.
Wisdom was mine, and I had mastery:
To miss the march of this retreating world
Into vain citadels that are not walled.
Then, when much blood had clogged their chariot-wheels,
I would go up and wash them from sweet wells,
Even with truths that lie too deep for taint.
I would have poured my spirit without stint

But not through wounds; not on the cess of war.
Foreheads of men have bled where no wounds were.
I am the enemy you killed, my friend.
I knew you in this dark; for so you frowned
Yesterday through me as you jabbed and killed.
I parried; but my hands were loath and cold.
Let us sleep now. . . .'

WILFRED OWEN
1893 – 1918

Bombardment

The Town has opened to the sun.
Like a flat red lily with a million petals
She unfolds, she comes undone.

A sharp sky brushes upon
The myriad glittering chimney-tops
As she gently exhales to the sun.

Hurrying creatures run
Down the labyrinth of the sinister flower.
What is it they shun?

A dark bird falls from the sun.
It curves in a rush to the heart of the vast
Flower: the day has begun.

D. H. LAWRENCE
1885 – 1930

The Dead in Europe

After the planes unloaded, we fell down
Buried together, unmarried men and women;
Not crown of thorns, not iron, not Lombard crown,
Not grilled and spindle spires pointing to heaven
Could save us. Raise us, Mother, we fell down
Here hugger-mugger in the jellied fire:
Our sacred earth in our day was our curse.

Our Mother, shall we rise on Mary's day
In Maryland, wherever corpses married
Under the rubble, bundled together? Pray
For us whom the blockbusters marred and buried;
When Satan scatters us on Rising-day,
O Mother, snatch our bodies from the fire:
Our sacred earth in our day was our curse.

Mother, my bones are trembling and I hear
The earth's reverberations and the trumpet
Bleating into my shambles. Shall I bear,
(O Mary!) unmarried man and powder-puppet,
Witness to the Devil? Mary, hear,
O Mary, marry earth, sea, air and fire;
Our sacred earth in our day is our curse.

ROBERT LOWELL
born 1917

A Sight in Camp

A sight in camp in the daybreak gray and dim,
As from my tent I emerge so early sleepless,
As slow I walk in the cool fresh air the path near by the
    hospital tent,
Three forms I see on stretchers lying, brought out there un-
    tended lying,
Over each the blanket spread, ample brownish woolen blanket,
Gray and heavy blanket, folding, covering all.

Curious I halt and silent stand,
Then with light fingers I from the face of the nearest the first
    just lift the blanket;
Who are you elderly man so gaunt and grim, with well-gray'd
    hair, and flesh all sunken about the eyes?
Who are you my dear comrade?

Then to the second I step – and who are you my child and
    darling?
Who are you sweet boy with cheeks yet blooming?

Then to the third – a face nor child nor old, very calm, as of
    beautiful yellow-white ivory;
Young man I think I know you – I think this face is the face of
    the Christ himself,
Dead and divine and brother of all, and here again he lies.

WALT WHITMAN
1819 – 1892

Peace

Sweet Peace, where dost thou dwell? I humbly crave,
      Let me once know.
   I sought thee in a secret cave,
    And ask'd if Peace were there.
A hollow wind did seem to answer, 'No;
      Go seek elsewhere.'

I did; and going did a rainbow note:
      Surely, thought I,
   This is the lace of Peace's coat:
    I will search out the matter.
But while I look'd, the clouds immediately
      Did break and scatter.

Then went I to a garden, and did spy
      A gallant flower,
   The crown Imperial. Sure, said I,
    Peace at the root must dwell.
But when I digg'd, I saw a worm devour
      What show'd so well.

At length I met a rev'rend good old man,
      Whom when for Peace
   I did demand, he thus began:
    'There was a Prince of old
At Salem dwelt, Who liv'd with good increase
      Of flock and fold.

'He sweetly liv'd; yet sweetness did not save
      His life from foes.
   But after death out of His grave
    There sprang twelve stalks of wheat;
Which many wond'ring at, got some of those
      To plant and set.

'It prosper'd strangely, and did soon disperse
      Through all the earth;
   For they that taste it do rehearse,
      That virtue lies therein;
A secret virtue, bringing peace and mirth
      By flight of sin.

'Take of this grain, which in my garden grows,
      And grows for you;
   Make bread of it; and that repose
      And peace, which ev'ry where
With so much earnestness you do pursue,
      Is only there.'

GEORGE HERBERT
1593 – 1632

Peace

   My Soul, there is a country
      Far beyond the stars,
   Where stands a wingèd sentry
      All skilful in the wars:
   There, above noise and danger,
      Sweet Peace sits crown'd with smiles,
   And One born in a manger
      Commands the beauteous files.
   He is thy gracious Friend,
      And – O my soul, awake! –
   Did in pure love descend
      To die here for thy sake.
   If thou canst get but thither,
      There grows the flower of Peace,
   The Rose that cannot wither,
      Thy fortress, and thy ease.
   Leave then thy foolish ranges;
      For none can thee secure
   But One who never changes –
      Thy God, thy Life, thy Cure.

HENRY VAUGHAN
1622 – 1695

Silence

There is a silence where hath been no sound,
  There is a silence where no sound may be,
  In the cold grave – under the deep, deep sea,
Or in wide desert where no life is found,
Which hath been mute, and still must sleep profound;
  No voice is hush'd – no life treads silently,
  But clouds and cloudy shadows wander free,
That never spoke, over the idle ground:
But in green ruins, in the desolate walls
  Of antique palaces, where Man hath been,
Though the dun fox, or wild hyaena, calls,
  And owls, that flit continually between,
Shriek to the echo, and the low winds moan –
There the true Silence is, self-conscious and alone.

THOMAS HOOD
1798 – 1845

Grass

Pile the bodies high at Austerlitz and Waterloo.
Shovel them under and let me work –
              I am the grass; I cover all.

And pile them high at Gettysburg,
And pile them high at Ypres and Verdun.
Shovel them under and let me work.
Two years, ten years, and passengers ask the conductor:
              What place is this?
              Where are we now?

              I am the grass.
              Let me work.

CARL SANDBURG
1878 – 1967

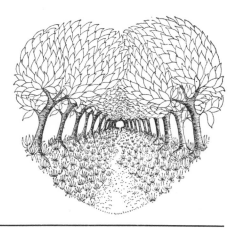

Friendship and love

The Passionate Shepherd
to His Love

Come live with me and be my Love,
And we will all the pleasures prove
That hills and valleys, dales and fields,
Or woods or steepy mountain yields.

And we will sit upon the rocks,
And see the shepherds feed their flocks
By shallow rivers, to whose falls
Melodious birds sing madrigals.

And I will make thee beds of roses
And a thousand fragrant posies;
A cap of flowers, and a kirtle
Embroider'd all with leaves of myrtle.

A gown made of the finest wool
Which from our pretty lambs we pull;
Fair-linèd slippers for the cold,
With buckles of the purest gold.

A belt of straw and ivy-buds
With coral clasps and amber studs:
And if these pleasures may thee move,
Come live with me and be my Love.

The shepherd swains shall dance and sing
For thy delight each May morning:
If these delights thy mind may move,
Then live with me and be my Love.

CHRISTOPHER MARLOWE
1564 – 1593

To –

One word is too often profaned
    For me to profane it;
One feeling too falsely disdain'd
    For thee to disdain it;
One hope is too like despair
    For prudence to smother;
And pity from thee more dear
    Than that from another.

I can give not what men call love;
    But wilt thou accept not
The worship the heart lifts above
    And the heavens reject not,
The desire of the moth for the star,
    Of the night for the morrow,
The devotion to something afar
    From the sphere of our sorrow?

PERCY BYSSHE SHELLEY
1792 – 1822

Love

Love bade me welcome: yet my soul drew back,
    Guiltie of dust and sinne.
But quick-ey'd Love, observing me grow slack
    From my first entrance in,
Drew nearer to me, sweetly questioning,
    If I lack'd any thing.

A guest, I answer'd, worthy to be here:
        Love said, you shall be he.
I the unkinde, ungratefull? Ah my deare,
        I cannot look on thee.
Love took my hand, and smiling did reply,
        Who made the eyes but I?

Truth Lord, but I have marr'd them: let my shame
        Go where it doth deserve.
And know you not, sayes Love, who bore the blame?
        My deare, then I will serve.
You must sit down, sayes Love, and taste my meat:
        So I did sit and eat.

GEORGE HERBERT
1593 – 1632

From the Bengali

Lord of my heart, what have I dreamed,
how shall I go home, now that daylight has come?
My musk and sandalwood perfumes are faded,
the kohl smudged from my eyes, the vermilion line
drawn in the part of my hair, paled.
O put the ornament
of your own body upon me,
take me with you, down-glancing one.
Dress me in your own yellow robes,
smooth my dishevelled hair,
wind round my throat your garland of forest flowers.
Thus, beloved, someone in Gokula entreats.

*Basu Ramananda says, Such is your love
that deer and tiger are together in your dwelling-place.*

Translated from the Bengali
by Edward C. Dimock, Jr. and Denise Levertov

71

A Birthday

My heart is like a singing bird
  Whose nest is in a water'd shoot;
My heart is like an apple-tree
  Whose boughs are bent with thick-set fruit;
My heart is like a rainbow shell
  That paddles in a halcyon sea;
My heart is gladder than all these,
  Because my love is come to me.

Raise me a daïs of silk and down;
  Hang it with vair and purple dyes;
Carve it in doves and pomegranates,
  And peacocks with a hundred eyes;
Work it in gold and silver grapes,
  In leaves and silver fleur-de-lys;
Because the birthday of my life
  Is come, my love is come to me.

CHRISTINA ROSSETTI
1830 – 1894

Monody

To have known him, to have loved him
  After loneness long;
And then to be estranged in life,
  And neither in the wrong;
And now for death to set his seal –
  Ease me, a little ease, my song!
By wintry hills his hermit-mound
  The sheeted snow-drifts drape,
And houseless there the snow-bird flits
  Beneath the fir-trees' crape:
Glazed now with ice the cloistral vine
  That hid the shyest grape.

HERMAN MELVILLE
1819 – 1891

My True Love Hath My Heart

My true love hath my heart, and I have his,
By just exchange one for another given:
I hold his dear, and mine he cannot miss,
There never was a better bargain driven:
My true love hath my heart, and I have his.

His heart in me keeps him and me in one,
My heart in him his thoughts and senses guides:
He loves my heart, for once it was his own,
I cherish his because in me it bides:
My true love hath my heart, and I have his.

SIR PHILIP SIDNEY
1554 – 1586

Like as a Huntsman after Weary Chase

Like as a huntsman after weary chase,
Seeing the game from him escaped away,
Sits down to rest him in some shady place,
With panting hounds beguilèd of their prey:
So, after long pursuit and vain assay,
When I all weary had the chase forsook,
The gentle deer returned the self-same way,
Thinking to quench her thirst at the next brook.
There she, beholding me with milder look,
Sought not to fly, but fearless still did bide:
Till I in hand her yet half trembling took,
And with her own good-will her firmly tied.
   Strange thing, me seemed, to see a beast so wild
   So goodly won, with her own will beguiled.

EDMUND SPENSER
1552 – 1599

Sonnet
Being Your Slave, What Should I Do But Tend

Being your slave, what should I do but tend
Upon the hours and times of your desire?
I have no precious time at all to spend,
Nor services to do, till you require.
Nor dare I chide the world-without-end hour
Whilst I, my sovereign, watch the clock for you,
Nor think the bitterness of absence sour
When you have bid your servant once adieu;
Nor dare I question with my jealous thought
Where you may be, or your affairs suppose,
But, like a sad slave, stay and think of nought
Save, where you are how happy you make those!
  So true a fool is love, that in your Will,
  Though you do any thing, he thinks no ill.

WILLIAM SHAKESPEARE
1564 – 1616

Song

How sweet I roam'd from field to field
And tasted all the summer's pride,
Till I the Prince of Love beheld
Who in the sunny beams did glide!

He show'd me lilies for my hair,
And blushing roses for my brow;
He led me through his gardens fair
Where all his golden pleasures grow.

With sweet May dews my wings were wet,
And Phoebus fir'd my vocal rage;
He caught me in his silken net,
And shut me in his golden cage.

He loves to sit and hear me sing,
Then, laughing, sports and plays with me;
Then stretches out my golden wing,
And mocks my loss of liberty.

WILLIAM BLAKE
1757 – 1827

The Visionary

Silent is the house: all are laid asleep;
One alone looks out o'er the snow-wreaths deep,
Watching every cloud, dreading every breeze
That whirls the 'wildering drift, and bends the groaning trees.

Cheerful is the hearth, soft the matted floor;
Not one shivering gust creeps through pane or door;
The little lamp burns straight, its rays shoot strong and far:
I trim it well, to be the wanderer's guiding-star.

Frown, my haughty sire! chide, my angry dame!
Set your slaves to spy; threaten me with shame:
But neither sire nor dame, nor prying serf shall know
What angel nightly tracks that waste of frozen snow.

What I love shall come like visitant of air,
Safe in secret power from lurking human snare;
Who loves me, no word of mine shall e'er betray,
Though for faith unstained my life must forfeit pay.

Burn then, little lamp; glimmer straight and clear –
Hush! a rustling wing stirs, methinks, the air:
He for whom I wait thus ever comes to me;
Strange Power! I trust thy might; trust thou my constancy.

EMILY BRONTË
1818 – 1848

When I Heard at the Close of the Day

When I heard at the close of the day how my name had been
    receiv'd with plaudits in the capitol, still it was not a
    happy night for me that follow'd,
And else when I carous'd, or when my plans were accomplish'd,
    still I was not happy,
But the day when I rose at dawn from the bed of perfect
    health, refresh'd, singing, inhaling the ripe breath of
    autumn,
When I saw the full moon in the west grow pale and disappear
    in the morning light,
When I wander'd alone over the beach, and undressing bathed,
    laughing with the cool waters, and saw the sun rise,
And when I thought how my dear friend my lover was on his
    way coming, O then I was happy,
O then each breath tasted sweeter, and all that day my food
    nourish'd me more, and the beautiful day pass'd well,
And the next came with equal joy, and with the next at
    evening came my friend,
And that night while all was still I heard the waters roll slowly
    continually up the shores,
I heard the hissing rustle of the liquid and sands as directed
    to me whispering to congratulate me,
For the one I love most lay sleeping by me under the same
    cover in the cool night,
In the stillness in the autumn moonbeams his face was inclined
    toward me,
And his arm lay lightly around my breast – and that night
    I was happy.

WALT WHITMAN
1819 – 1892

76

With Rue My Heart Is Laden

With rue my heart is laden
   For golden friends I had,
For many a rose-lipt maiden
   And many a lightfoot lad.

By brooks too broad for leaping
   The lightfoot boys are laid;
The rose-lipt girls are sleeping
   In fields where roses fade.

A. E. HOUSMAN
1859 – 1936

A Poison Tree

I was angry with my friend:
I told my wrath, my wrath did end.
I was angry with my foe:
I told it not, my wrath did grow.

And I water'd it in fears,
Night and morning with my tears;
And I sunned it with smiles,
And with soft deceitful wiles.

And it grew both day and night,
Till it bore an apple bright;
And my foe beheld it shine,
And he knew that it was mine,

And into my garden stole
When the night had veil'd the pole:
In the morning glad I see
My foe outstretch'd beneath the tree.

WILLIAM BLAKE
1757 – 1827

To –

I fear thy kisses, gentle maiden,
    Thou needest not fear mine;
My spirit is too deeply laden
    Ever to burthen thine.

I fear thy mien, thy tones, thy motion,
    Thou needest not fear mine;
Innocent is the heart's devotion
    With which I worship thine.

PERCY BYSSHE SHELLEY
1792 – 1822

Sonnet
Shall I Compare Thee to a Summer's Day?

Shall I compare thee to a Summer's day?
Thou art more lovely and more temperate:
Rough winds do shake the darling buds of May,
And Summer's lease hath all too short a date:
Sometime too hot the eye of heaven shines,
And often is his gold complexion dimm'd;
And every fair from fair sometime declines,
By chance or nature's changing course untrimm'd:
But thy eternal Summer shall not fade
Nor lose possession of that fair thou owest;
Nor shall Death brag thou wanderest in his shade,
When in eternal lines to time thou growest:
    So long as men can breathe, or eyes can see,
    So long lives this, and this gives life to thee.

WILLIAM SHAKESPEARE
1564 – 1616

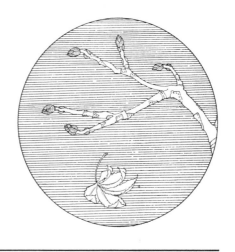

Death

The Last Journey

With courage seek the kingdom of the dead;
The path before you lies,
It is not hard to find, nor tread;
No rocks to climb, no lanes to thread;
But broad, and straight, and even still,
And ever gently slopes down-hill;
You cannot miss it, though you shut your eyes.

LEONIDAS OF TARENTUM
3rd Century B.C.
Translated from the Ancient Greek
by Charles Merivale

Inexorable

My thoughts hold mortal strife;
I do detest my life,
And with lamenting cries,
Peace to my soul to bring
Oft call that prince which here doth monarchize:
– But he, grim-grinning King,
Who caitiffs scorns, and doth the blest surprise,
Late having deck'd with beauty's rose his tomb,
Disdains to crop a weed, and will not come.

WILLIAM DRUMMOND, OF HAWTHORNDEN
1585 – 1649

Dirge
From *Twelfth Night*

Come away, come away, death,
  And in sad cypress let me be laid;
Fly away, fly away, breath;
  I am slain by a fair cruel maid.
My shroud of white, stuck all with yew,
      O prepare it!
My part of death, no one so true
      Did share it.

Not a flower, not a flower sweet,
  On my black coffin let there be strown;
Not a friend, not a friend greet
  My poor corse, where my bones shall be thrown:
A thousand thousand sighs to save,
      Lay me, O, where
Sad true lover never find my grave
      To weep there!

WILLIAM SHAKESPEARE
1564 – 1616

Vitae Summa Brevis Spem Nos Vetat
Incohare Longam

They are not long, the weeping and the laughter,
  Love and desire and hate:
I think they have no portion in us after
  We pass the gate.

They are not long, the days of wine and roses:
  Out of a misty dream
Our path emerges for a while, then closes
  Within a dream.

ERNEST DOWSON
1867 – 1900

The Watch

I wakened on my hot, hard bed,
Upon the pillow lay my head;
Beneath the pillow I could hear
My little watch was ticking clear.
I thought the throbbing of it went
Like my continual discontent;
I thought it said in every tick:
I am so sick, so sick, so sick:
O death, come quick, come quick, come quick,
Come quick, come quick, come quick, come quick.

FRANCES CORNFORD
1886 – 1960

I Heard a Fly Buzz When I Died

I heard a fly buzz when I died;
  The stillness round my form
Was like the stillness in the air
  Between the heaves of storm.

The eyes beside had wrung them dry,
  And breaths were gathering sure
For that last onset, when the king
  Be witnessed in his power.

I willed my keepsakes, signed away
  What portion of me I
Could make assignable, – and then
  There interposed a fly,

With blue, uncertain, stumbling buzz,
  Between the light and me;
And then the windows failed, and then
  I could not see to see.

EMILY DICKINSON
1830 – 1886

83

Kevin Barry:
Died for Ireland, 1st November 1920

In Mountjoy jail one Monday morning,
High upon the gallows tree
Kevin Barry gave his young life,
For the cause of liberty,
But a lad of eighteen summers,
Yet no one can deny
As he walked to death that morning,
He proudly held his head on high.

Just before he faced the hangman,
In his dreary prison cell,
British soldiers tortured Barry,
Just because he would not tell
The names of his brave companions,
And other things they wished to know,
'Turn informer or we'll kill you,'
Kevin Barry answered 'No.'

Calmly standing to 'attention',
While he bade his last farewell
To his broken-hearted mother,
Whose grief no one can tell.
For the cause he proudly cherished,
This sad parting had to be;
Then to death walked softly smiling,
That old Ireland might be free.

Another martyr for old Ireland,
Another murder for the crown,
Whose brutal laws may kill the Irish,
But can't keep their spirit down.
Lads like Barry are no cowards,
From the foe they will not fly,
Lads like Barry will free Ireland,
For her sake they'll live and die.

ANON.

To Hang a Man

To hang a man:
To fit the cap,
And fix the rope,
And slide the bar,
And let him drop.
I know, I know:
What can you do!
You have no choice,
You're driven to;
You can't be soft –
A man like that;
But Oh it seems –
I don't know what –
To hang a man!

RALPH HODGSON
1871 – 1962

Eight O'Clock

He stood, and heard the steeple
 Sprinkle the quarters on the morning town.
One, two, three, four, to market-place and people
 It tossed them down.

Strapped, noosed, nighing his hour,
 He stood and counted them and cursed his luck;
And then the clock collected in the tower
 Its strength, and struck.

A. E. HOUSMAN
1859 – 1936

Who Were before Me

Long time in some forgotten churchyard earth of Warwick-
    shire,
My fathers in their generations lie beyond desire,
And nothing breaks the rest, I know, of John Drinkwater now,
Who left in sixteen-seventy his roan team at plough.

And James, son of John, is there, a mighty ploughman too.
Skilled he was at thatching and the barleycorn brew,
And he had a heart-load of sorrow in his day,
But ten score of years ago he put it away.

Then Thomas came, and played a fiddle cut of mellow wood,
And broke his heart, they say, for love that never came to good.
A hundred winter peals and more have rung above his bed –
O, poor eternal grief, so long, so lightly, comforted.

And in the gentle yesterday these were but glimmering tombs,
Or tales to tell on fireside eves of legendary dooms;
I being life while they were none, what had their dust to bring
But cold intelligence of death upon my tides of Spring?

Now grief is in my shadow, and it seems well enough
To be there with my fathers, where neither fear nor love
Can touch me more, nor spite of men, nor my own teasing
    blame,
While the slow mosses weave an end of my forgotten name.

JOHN DRINKWATER
1882 – 1937

To an Athlete Dying Young

The time you won your town the race
We chaired you through the market-place;
Man and boy stood cheering by,
And home we brought you shoulder-high.

Today, the road all runners come,
Shoulder-high we bring you home,
And set you at your threshold down,
Townsman of a stiller town.

Smart lad, to slip betimes away
From fields where glory does not stay
And early though the laurel grows
It withers quicker than the rose.

Eyes the shady night has shut
Cannot see the record cut,
And silence sounds no worse than cheers
After earth has stopped the ears:

Now you will not swell the rout
Of lads that wore their honours out,
Runners whom renown outran
And the name died before the man.

So set, before its echoes fade,
The fleet foot on the sill of shade,
And hold to the low lintel up
The still-defended challenge-cup.

And round that early-laurelled head
Will flock to gaze the strengthless dead,
And find unwithered on its curls
The garland briefer than a girl's.

A. E. HOUSMAN
1859 – 1936

Success Is Counted Sweetest

Success is counted sweetest
By those who ne'er succeed.
To comprehend a nectar
Requires sorest need.

Not one of all the purple host
Who took the flag today
Can tell the definition,
So clear, of victory,

As he, defeated, dying,
On whose forbidden ear
The distant strains of triumph
Break, agonized and clear.

EMILY DICKINSON
1830 – 1886

Requiescat

Tread lightly, she is near
    Under the snow,
Speak gently, she can hear
    The daisies grow.

All her bright golden hair
    Tarnished with rust,
She that was young and fair
    Fallen to dust.

Lily-like, white as snow,
  She hardly knew
She was a woman, so
  Sweetly she grew.

Coffin-board, heavy stone,
  Lie on her breast,
I vex my heart alone,
  She is at rest.

Peace, Peace, she cannot hear
  Lyre or sonnet,
All my life's buried here,
  Heap earth upon it.

OSCAR WILDE
1854 – 1900

Sonnet
No Longer Mourn for Me When I am Dead

No longer mourn for me when I am dead,
Than you shall hear the surly sullen bell
Give warning to the world that I am fled
From this vile world, with vilest worms to dwell:
Nay, if you read this line, remember not
The hand that writ it; for I love you so,
That I in your sweet thoughts would be forgot,
If thinking on me then should make you woe.
O! if, I say, you look upon this verse,
When I perhaps compounded am with clay,
Do not so much as my poor name rehearse,
But let your love even with my life decay;
  Lest the wise world should look into your moan,
  And mock you with me after I am gone.

WILLIAM SHAKESPEARE
1564 – 1616

Is My Team Ploughing

'Is my team ploughing,
  That I was used to drive
And hear the harness jingle
  When I was man alive?'

Ay, the horses trample,
  The harness jingles now;
No change though you lie under
  The land you used to plough.

'Is football playing
  Along the river shore,
With lads to chase the leather,
  Now I stand up no more?'

Ay, the ball is flying,
  The lads play heart and soul;
The goal stands up, the keeper
  Stands up to keep the goal.

'Is my girl happy,
  That I thought hard to leave,
And has she tired of weeping
  As she lies down at eve?'

Ay, she lies down lightly,
  She lies not down to weep:
Your girl is well contented.
  Be still, my lad, and sleep.

'Is my friend hearty,
  Now I am thin and pine,
And has he found to sleep in
  A better bed than mine?'

Yes, lad, I lie easy,
  I lie as lads would choose;
I cheer a dead man's sweetheart,
  Never ask me whose.

A. E. HOUSMAN
1859 – 1936

90

A Slumber

A slumber did my spirit seal;
  I had no human fears:
She seem'd a thing that could not feel
  The touch of earthly years.

No motion has she now, no force;
  She neither hears nor sees;
Roll'd round in earth's diurnal course,
  With rocks, and stones, and trees.

WILLIAM WORDSWORTH
1770 – 1850

'Biby's' Epitaph

A muvver was barfin' 'er biby one night,
The youngest of ten and a tiny young mite,
The muvver was poor and the biby was thin,
Only a skelington covered in skin;
The muvver turned rahnd for the soap off the rack,
She was but a moment, but when she turned back,
The biby was gorn; and in anguish she cried,
'Oh, where is my biby?' – The angels replied:

'Your biby 'as fell dahn the plug-'ole,
Your biby 'as gorn dahn the plug;
The poor little thing was so skinny and thin
'E oughter been barfed in a jug;
Your biby is perfeckly 'appy,
'E won't need a barf any more,
Your biby 'as fell dahn the plug-'ole,
Not lorst, but gorn before.'

ANON.

Horace Paraphrased

There are a number of us creep
Into this world to eat and sleep,
And know no reason why they're born
But merely to consume the corn,
Devour the cattle, fowl and fish,
And leave behind an empty dish.
The crows and ravens do the same,
Unlucky birds of hateful name;
Ravens or crows might fill their place,
And swallow corn and carcases.
Then if their tombstone when they die
Ben't taught to flatter and to lie,
There's nothing better will be said
Than that 'They've eat up all their bread,
Drank up their drink and gone to bed.'

ISAAC WATTS
1674 – 1748

The Conclusion

Even such is Time, that takes in trust
Our youth, our joys, our all we have,
And pays us but with earth and dust;
Who in the dark and silent grave,
When we have wander'd all our ways,
Shuts up the story of our days;
But from this earth, this grave, this dust,
My God shall raise me up, I trust.

SIR WALTER RALEIGH
1552 – 1618

Dreams and enchantments

A Dream within a Dream

Take this kiss upon the brow!
And, in parting from you now,
Thus much let me avow:
You are not wrong, who deem
That my days have been a dream;
Yet if Hope has flown away
In a night, or in a day,
In a vision, or in none,
Is it therefore the less *gone*?
All that we see or seem
Is but a dream within a dream.

I stand amid the roar
Of a surf-tormented shore,
And I hold within my hand
Grains of the golden sand –
How few! yet how they creep
Through my fingers to the deep,
While I weep – while I weep!
O God! can I not grasp
Them with a tighter clasp?
O God! can I not save
One from the pitiless wave?
Is *all* that we see or seem
But a dream within a dream?

EDGAR ALLAN POE
1809 – 1849

Dream and Poetry

It's all ordinary experience,
All ordinary images.
By chance they emerge in a dream,
Turning out infinite new patterns.

It's all ordinary feelings,
All ordinary words.
By chance they encounter a poet,
Turning out infinite new verses.

Once intoxicated, one learns the strength of wine,
Once smitten, one learns the power of love:
You cannot write my poems
Just as I cannot dream your dreams.

HU SHIH
1891 – 1962
*Translated from the Chinese
by Kai-Yu Hsu*

Aedh Wishes for the Cloths of Heaven

Had I the heavens' embroidered cloths,
Enwrought with golden and silver light,
The blue and the dim and the dark cloths
Of night and light and the half-light,
I would spread the cloths under your feet:
But I, being poor, have only my dreams;
I have spread my dreams under your feet;
Tread softly because you tread on my dreams.

WILLIAM BUTLER YEATS
1865 – 1939

From A Midsummer Night's Dream

I know a bank whereon the wild thyme blows,
Where oxlips and the nodding violet grows;
Quite over-canopied with lush woodbine,
With sweet musk-roses, and with eglantine:
There sleeps Titania, sometime of the night,
Lull'd in these flowers with dances and delight;
And there the snake throws her enamell'd skin,
Weed wide enough to wrap a fairy in.

WILLIAM SHAKESPEARE
1564 – 1616

Sudden Light

I have been here before
   But when or how I cannot tell:
I know the grass beyond the door,
   The sweet keen smell,
The sighing sound, the lights around the shore.

You have been mine before, –
   How long ago I may not know:
But just when at that swallow's soar
   Your neck turned so,
Some veil did fall, – I knew it all of yore.

Has this been thus before?
   And shall not thus time's eddying flight
Still with our lives our love restore
   In death's despite,
And day and night yield one delight once more?

DANTE GABRIEL ROSSETTI
1828 – 1882

G

The Fairy Blessing

From *A Midsummer Night's Dream*

Puck: Now the hungry lion roars,
        And the wolf behowls the moon;
    Whilst the heavy ploughman snores,
        All with weary task fordone.
    Now the wasted brands do glow,
        Whilst the screech-owl, screeching loud,
    Puts the wretch that lies in woe
        In remembrance of a shroud.
    Now it is the time of night
        That the graves, all gaping wide,
    Every one lets forth his sprite,
        In the church-way paths to glide:
    And we fairies, that do run
        By the triple Hecate's team,
    From the presence of the sun,
        Following darkness like a dream,
    Now are frolic; not a mouse
    Shall disturb this hallow'd house:
    I am sent with broom before,
    To sweep the dust behind the door.

Oberon: Through the house give glimmering light
        By the dead and drowsy fire;
    Every elf and fairy sprite
        Hop as light as bird from briar;
    And this ditty after me
    Sing, and dance it trippingly.

Titania: First, rehearse your song by rote.
    To each word a warbling note.
    Hand in hand, with fairy grace,
    Will we sing, and bless this place.

Oberon: Now, until the break of day,
    Through this house each fairy stray.
    To the best bride-bed will we,
    Which by us shall blessed be;

And the issue there create
Ever shall be fortunate.
So shall all the couples three
Ever true in loving be;
And the blots of Nature's hand
Shall not in their issue stand:
Never mole, hare-lip, nor scar,
Nor mark prodigious, such as are
Despised in nativity,
Shall upon their children be.
With this field-dew consecrate,
Every fairy take his gait,
And each several chamber bless,
Through this palace, with sweet peace,
And the owner of it blest
Ever shall in safety rest.

WILLIAM SHAKESPEARE
1564 – 1616

La Belle Dame Sans Merci

'O what can ail thee, knight-at-arms,
    Alone and palely loitering?
The sedge is wither'd from the lake,
    And no birds sing.

'O what can ail thee, knight-at-arms,
    So haggard and so woe-begone?
The squirrel's granary is full,
    And the harvest's done.

'I see a lily on thy brow
    With anguish moist and fever dew;
And on thy cheeks a fading rose
    Fast withereth too.'

'I met a lady in the meads,
    Full beautiful – a faery's child,
Her hair was long, her foot was light,
    And her eyes were wild.

'I made a garland for her head,
   And bracelets too, and fragrant zone;
She look'd at me as she did love,
   And made sweet moan.

'I set her on my pacing steed
   And nothing else saw all day long,
For sideways would she lean, and sing
   A faery's song.

'She found me roots of relish sweet,
   And honey wild, and manna dew,
And sure in language strange she said,
   "I love thee true."

'She took me to her elfin grot,
   And there she wept and sigh'd full sore,
And there I shut her wild, wild eyes
   With kisses four.

'And there she lullèd me asleep,
   And there I dream'd – Ah! woe betide!
The latest dream I ever dream'd
   On the cold hill's side.

'I saw pale kings and princes too,
   Pale warriors, death-pale were they all;
They cried – "La belle Dame sans Merci
   Hath thee in thrall!"

'I saw their starved lips in the gloam
   With horrid warning gapèd wide,
And I awoke and found me here
   On the cold hill's side.

'And this is why I sojourn here
   Alone and palely loitering,
Though the sedge is wither'd from the lake
   And no birds sing.'

JOHN KEATS
1795 – 1821

Kubla Khan

In Xanadu did Kubla Khan
A stately pleasure-dome decree:
Where Alph, the sacred river, ran
Through caverns measureless to man
   Down to a sunless sea.
So twice five miles of fertile ground
With walls and towers were girdled round:
And there were gardens bright with sinuous rills,
Where blossomed many an incense-bearing tree;
And here were forests ancient as the hills,
Enfolding sunny spots of greenery.

But oh! that deep romantic chasm which slanted
Down the green hill athwart a cedarn cover!
A savage place! as holy and enchanted
As e'er beneath a waning moon was haunted
By woman wailing for her demon-lover!
And from this chasm, with ceaseless turmoil seething,
As if this earth in fast thick pants were breathing,
A mighty fountain momently was forced:
Amid whose swift half-intermitted burst
Huge fragments vaulted like rebounding hail,
Or chaffy grain beneath the thresher's flail:
And 'mid these dancing rocks at once and ever
It flung up momently the sacred river.
Five miles meandering with a mazy motion
Through wood and dale the sacred river ran,
Then reached the caverns measureless to man,
And sank in tumult to a lifeless ocean:
And 'mid this tumult Kubla heard from far
Ancestral voices prophesying war!

   The shadow of the dome of pleasure
   Floated midway on the waves;
   Where was heard the mingled measure
   From the fountain and the caves.
It was a miracle of rare device,
A sunny pleasure-dome with caves of ice!

A damsel with a dulcimer
In a vision once I saw:
It was an Abyssinian maid,
And on her dulcimer she played,
Singing of Mount Abora.
Could I revive within me
Her symphony and song,
To such a deep delight 'twould win me,
That with music loud and long,
I would build that dome in air,
That sunny dome! those caves of ice!
And all who heard should see them there,
And all should cry, Beware! Beware!
His flashing eyes, his floating hair!
Weave a circle round him thrice,
And close your eyes with holy dread,
For he on honey-dew hath fed,
And drunk the milk of Paradise.

SAMUEL TAYLOR COLERIDGE
1772 – 1834

The Stolen Child

Where dips the rocky highland
Of Sleuth Wood in the lake,
There lies a leafy island
Where flapping herons wake
The drowsy water-rats;
There we've hid our faery vats,
Full of berries
And of reddest stolen cherries.
Come away, O human child!
To the waters and the wild
With a faery, hand in hand,
For the world's more full of weeping than
    you can understand.

Where the wave of moonlight glosses
The dim grey sands with light,
Far off by furthest Rosses
We foot it all the night,

Weaving olden dances,
Mingling hands and mingling glances
Till the moon has taken flight;
To and fro we leap
And chase the frothy bubbles,
While the world is full of troubles
And is anxious in its sleep.
Come away, O human child!
To the waters and the wild
With a faery, hand in hand,
For the world's more full of weeping than
*   you can understand.*

Where the wandering water gushes
From the hills above Glen-Car,
In pools among the rushes
That scarce could bathe a star,
We seek for slumbering trout
And whispering in their ears
Give them unquiet dreams;
Leaning softly out
From ferns that drop their tears
Over the young streams.
Come away, O human child!
To the waters and the wild
With a faery, hand in hand,
For the world's more full of weeping than
*   you can understand.*

Away with us he's going,
The solemn-eyed:
He'll hear no more the lowing
Of the calves on the warm hillside
Or the kettle on the hob
Sing peace into his breast,
Or see the brown mice bob
Round and round the oatmeal-chest.
For he comes, the human child,
To the waters and the wild
With a faery, hand in hand,
From a world more full of weeping than
*   he can understand.*

WILLIAM BUTLER YEATS
1865 – 1939

Fancy

Ever let the Fancy roam,
Pleasure never is at home:
At a touch sweet Pleasure melteth,
Like to bubbles when rain pelteth;
Then let wingèd Fancy wander
Through the thought still spread beyond her:
Open wide the mind's cage-door,
She'll dart forth, and cloudward soar.
O sweet Fancy! let her loose;
Summer's joys are spoilt by use,
And the enjoying of the Spring
Fades as does its blossoming:
Autumn's red-lipp'd fruitage too,
Blushing through the mist and dew,
Cloys with tasting: What do then?
Sit thee by the ingle, when
The sear faggot blazes bright,
Spirit of a winter's night;
When the soundless earth is muffled,
And the cakèd snow is shuffled
From the ploughboy's heavy shoon;
When the Night doth meet the Noon
In a dark conspiracy
To banish Even from her sky.
Sit thee there, and send abroad,
With a mind self-overawed,
Fancy, high-commission'd: – send her!
She has vassals to attend her:
She will bring, in spite of frost,
Beauties that the earth hath lost;
She will bring thee, all together,
All delights of summer weather;
All the buds and bells of May,
From dewy sward or thorny spray;
All the heapèd Autumn's wealth,
With a still, mysterious stealth:
She will mix these pleasures up
Like three fit wines in a cup,
And thou shalt quaff it: – thou shalt hear
Distant harvest-carols clear;

Rustle of the reapèd corn;
Sweet birds antheming the morn:
And in the same moment – hark!
'Tis the early April lark,
Or the rooks, with busy caw,
Foraging for sticks and straw.
Thou shalt, at one glance behold
The daisy and the marigold;
White-plumed lilies, and the first
Hedge-grown primrose that hath burst;
Shaded hyacinth, alway
Sapphire queen of the mid-May;
And every leaf, and every flower
Pearlèd with the self-same shower.
Thou shalt see the fieldmouse peep
Meagre from its cellèd sleep;
And the snake all winter-thin
Cast on sunny bank its skin;
Freckled nest-eggs thou shalt see
Hatching in the hawthorn-tree,
When the hen-bird's wing doth rest
Quiet on her mossy nest;
Then the hurry and alarm
When the beehive casts its swarm;
Acorns ripe down-pattering
While the autumn breezes sing.

O sweet Fancy! let her loose;
Every thing is spoilt by use:
Where's the cheek that doth not fade,
Too much gazed at? Where's the maid
Whose lip mature is ever new?
Where's the eye, however blue,
Doth not weary? Where's the face
One would meet in every place?
Where's the voice, however soft,
One would hear so very oft?
At a touch sweet Pleasure melteth
Like to bubbles when rain pelteth.
Let, then, wingèd Fancy find

Thee a mistress to thy mind:
Dulcet-eyed as Ceres' daughter,
Ere the God of Torment taught her
How to frown and how to chide;
With a waist and with a side
White as Hebe's, when her zone
Slipt its golden clasp, and down
Fell her kirtle to her feet,
While she held the goblet sweet,
And Jove grew languid. – Break the mesh
Of the Fancy's silken leash;
Quickly break her prison-string,
And such joys as these she'll bring. –
Let the wingèd Fancy roam,
Pleasure never is at home.

JOHN KEATS
1795 – 1821

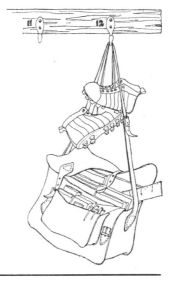

Work and play

The Ricksha Puller

In motion, perpetually in motion, are his legs
Running in this world of suffering, like the everflowing water.
He strikes a stance beyond suffering, his sense of pain has long
    fallen asleep.
Despite the passage of time, he still can hold himself erect
As a perfect embodiment of the patience of this ancient land.

Who is racing with him?
Death, death wants to embrace
This Marathon runner racing with life.
If he loses, death will seize him;
If he wins, no triumphal march will be heard.
A breeze stirs on the sea, saying
This is a shameful strange sight;
It must be erased by the ingenuity of man.
Thus, the strength of man's body, an ancient glory,
Has been turned into a modern disgrace.

The storms in the sky, the rugged roads on earth,
The direction of departure in the morning, the route of return
    at night.
All lie beyond his prediction, his design.
His answer is only an unbreakable silence.
The wishes of the people on the road drive him,
His own wishes are tossed on the roadside.
An aimless man lives to fulfill the wishes of others.

Every time he stops,
Still panting, he stretches out his dirty hands.
(Please reflect, reflect, I beg of you:
Beneath this dirty skin flows clean blood
While in those clean fingers flows dirty blood.
Which is our shame:
The dirty blood, or the dirty hands?)
With his worn feet he opens up for you
The roads leading to innumerable different destinations.
(After having your innumerable purposes fulfilled, would you
    also
Think of a way out for his purpose that has lain long
    smothered?)

It's not that there is no way, there is a way,
And it has become the prayer of all men;
It is waiting in the dim distance
For all our hands, all our feet
Both the hungry and the well-fed, to remove
The spreading weeds, and to tread out a smooth road.
In motion, forever in motion are his legs
Running along a road that begins and ends with life.
In the wind of winter, the rain of hunger, and the thunder and
    lightning of death,
Moving, forever moving are his legs.

CHENG MIN
born 1924
Translated from the Chinese
by Kai-Yu Hsu

The Astronaut

Star-sailor, with your eyes on space,
You map an ocean in the sky at night.
I see you stride with scientific grace
Upon the crusted suns of yesterday
As if it were tomorrow, in the place
Of time, the voyager beyond this momentary stay
Whose loaded instruments of light
Shoot rocket-galaxies around the bend of sight.

JAMES KIRKUP
born 1923

The Song of the Shirt

With fingers weary and worn,
  With eyelids heavy and red,
A Woman sat, in unwomanly rags,
  Plying her needle and thread –
    Stitch! stitch! stitch!
In poverty, hunger, and dirt,
And still with a voice of dolorous pitch
She sang the 'Song of the Shirt!'

'Work! work! work!
While the cock is crowing aloof!
  And work – work – work,
Till the stars shine through the roof!
It's O! to be a slave
  Along with the barbarous Turk,
Where woman has never a soul to save,
  If this is Christian work!

'Work – work – work
Till the brain begins to swim;
  Work – work – work
Till the eyes are heavy and dim!
Seam, and gusset, and band,
  Band, and gusset, and seam,
Till over the buttons I fall asleep,
  And sew them on in a dream!

'O, Men with Sisters dear!
  O, Men! with Mothers and Wives!
It is not linen you're wearing out,
  But human creatures' lives!
    Stitch – stitch – stitch,
  In poverty, hunger, and dirt,
Sewing at once, with a double thread,
  A Shroud as well as a Shirt.

'But why do I talk of Death?
  That Phantom of grisly bone,
I hardly fear his terrible shape,
  It seems so like my own –
  It seems so like my own,
  Because of the fasts I keep;
O God! that bread should be so dear,
  And flesh and blood so cheap!

'Work – work – work!
  My labour never flags;
And what are its wages? A bed of straw,
  A crust of bread – and rags.
That shatter'd roof, – and this naked floor –
  A table – a broken chair –
And a wall so blank, my shadow I thank
  For sometimes falling there!

'Work – work – work!
From weary chime to chime,
  Work – work – work –
As prisoners work for crime!
  Band, and gusset, and seam,
  Seam, and gusset, and band,
Till the heart is sick, and the brain benumb'd,
  As well as the weary hand.

'Work – work – work,
In the dull December light,
  And work – work – work,
When the weather is warm and bright –
While underneath the eaves
  The brooding swallows cling
As if to show me their sunny backs
  And twit me with the spring.

'O, but to breathe the breath
Of the cowslip and primrose sweet! –
   With the sky above my head,
And the grass beneath my feet;
For only one short hour
   To feel as I used to feel,
Before I knew the woes of want
   And the walk that costs a meal!

'O, but for one short hour!
   A respite however brief!
No blessed leisure for Love or Hope,
   But only time for Grief!
A little weeping would ease my heart,
   But in their briny bed
My tears must stop, for every drop
   Hinders needle and thread!'

'Seam, and gusset, and band,
Band, and gusset, and seam,
   Work, work, work,
Like the Engine that works by Steam!
A mere machine of iron and wood
   That toils for Mammon's sake –
Without a brain to ponder and craze
   Or a heart to feel – and break!'

– With fingers weary and worn,
   With eyelids heavy and red,
   A Woman sat, in unwomanly rags,
   Plying her needle and thread –
      Stitch! stitch! stitch!
   In poverty, hunger, and dirt,
And still with a voice of dolorous pitch, –
Would that its tone could reach the Rich! –
   She sang this 'Song of the Shirt!'

THOMAS HOOD
1798 – 1845

The Laundry Song

(One piece, two pieces, three pieces,)
Washing must be clean.
(Four pieces, five pieces, six pieces,)
Ironing must be smooth.

I can wash handkerchiefs wet with sad tears;
I can wash shirts soiled in sinful crimes.
The grease of greed, the dirt of desire . . .
And all the filthy things at your house,
Give them to me to wash, give them to me.

Brass stinks so; blood smells evil.
Dirty things you have to wash.
Once washed, they will again be soiled.
How can you, men of patience, ignore them!
Wash them (for the Americans), wash them!

You say the laundry business is too base.
Only Chinamen are willing to stoop so low?
It was your preacher who once told me:
Christ's father used to be a carpenter.
Do you believe it? Don't you believe it?

There isn't much you can do with soap and water.
Washing clothes truly can't compare with building warships.
I, too, say what great prospect lies in this –
Washing the others' sweat with your own blood and sweat?
(But) do you want to do it? Do you want it?

Year in year out a drop of homesick tears;
Midnight, in the depth of night, a laundry lamp . . .
Menial or not, you need not bother,
Just see what is not clean, what is not smooth,
And ask the Chinaman, ask the Chinaman.

I can wash handkerchiefs wet with sad tears,
I can wash shirts soiled in sinful crimes.
The grease of greed, the dirt of desire . . .
And all the filthy things at your house,
Give them to me – I'll wash them, give them to me!

WEN I-TO
1899 – 1946
*Translated from the Chinese
by Kai-Yu Hsu*

From **Windsor Forest**

In genial spring, beneath the quivering shade,
Where cooling vapours breathe along the mead,
The patient fisher takes his silent stand,
Intent, his angle trembling in his hand:
With looks unmoved, he hopes the scaly breed,
And eyes the dancing cork, and bending reed.
Our plenteous streams a various race supply,
The bright-eyed perch with fins of Tyrian dye,
The silver eel, in shining volumes roll'd,
The yellow carp, in scales bedropp'd with gold,
Swift trouts, diversified with crimson stains,
And pikes, the tyrants of the watery plains.

ALEXANDER POPE
1688–1744

In a Sailplane

Still as a bird
Transfixed in flight
We shiver and flow
Into leagues of light.

Rising and turning
Without a sound
As summer lifts us
Off the ground.

The sky's deep bell
Of glass rings down.
We slip in a sea
That cannot drown.

We kick the wide
Horizon's blues
Like a cluttering hoop
From round our shoes.

This easy 'plane
So quietly speaks,
Like a tree it sighs
In silvery shrieks.

Neatly we soar
Through a roaring cloud:
Its caverns of snow
Are dark and loud.

Into banks of sun
Above the drifts
Of quilted cloud
Our stillness shifts.

Here no curious
Bird comes near.
We float alone
In a snowman's sphere.

Higher than spires
Where breath is rare
We beat the shires
Of racing air.

Up the cliff
Of sheer no-place
We swarm a rope
That swings on space.

Breezed by a star's
Protracted stare
We watch the earth
Drop out of air.

Red stars of light
Burn on the round
Of land: street-constellations
Strew the ground.

Their bridges leap
From town to town:
Into lighted dusk
We circle down.

Still as a bird
Transfixed in flight
We come to nest
In the field of night.

JAMES KIRKUP
born 1923

Kite-Flying at Kobe

The kites blow upward, golden dragons, birds,
Darting across the scroll-work of the sky . . .
The children laugh and dance there as they fly
More plenteous than love, better than words.

O see those wild things in their heaven-dance!
Dazzling the eyes, giving the heart release!
And in their journey know an hour of peace
Held in the golden magic of a trance,

A child again, walking the courts of air,
Furling enchanted wings, knowing the skin
Of sorrow fallen from the bones, the din
Of Kobe like a rushing river there!

It lasts a while, then from a schoolboy's hand
One brilliant kite is snatched, and floats away,
Across the tiles, those dragon-scales of day,
And settles on the thin and drifting sand.

The sea takes it; now like a broken sail
Sucked by the receding tide, it goes
Outward and outward where the tempest blows;
The dream is over where the sea-birds wail.

CHARLES HIGHAM
born 1931

Evening – Regatta Day

Your nose is a red jelly, your mouth's a toothless wreck,
And I'm atop of you, banging your head upon the dirty deck;
And both your eyes are bunged and blind like those of a
    mewling pup,
For you're the juggins who caught the crab and lost the ship
    the Cup.

He caught a crab in the spurt home, this blushing cherub did,
And the *Craigie's* whaler slipped ahead like a cart-wheel on the
    skid,
And beat us fair by the boat's nose though we sweated fit to
    start her,
So we are playing at Nero now, and *he's* the Christian martyr.

And Stroke is lashing a bunch of keys to the buckle-end of a
    belt,
And we're going to lay you over a chest and baste you till you
    melt.
The *Craigie* boys are beating the bell and cheering down the
    tier,
D'ye hear, you Port Mahone baboon, I ask you, do you *hear*?

JOHN MASEFIELD
1878 – 1967

Man Carrying Bale

The tough hand closes gently on the load;
   Out of the mind, a voice
Calls 'Lift!' and the arms, remembering well their work,
   Lengthen and pause for help.
Then a slow ripple flows along the body,
While all the muscles call to one another:
   'Lift!' and the bulging bale
   Floats like a butterfly in June.

So moved the earliest carrier of bales,
   And the same watchful sun
Glowed through his body feeding it with light.
   So will the last one move,
And halt, and dip his head, and lay his load
Down, and the muscles will relax and tremble . . .
   Earth, you designed your man
Beautiful both in labour, and repose.

HAROLD MONRO
1879 – 1932

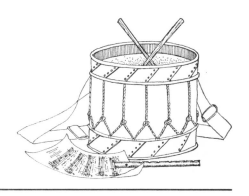

Music and songs

Song of the Young

Some people don't know
That their day's nearly gone,
Some people don't know
That their world's running down,
Some people don't know
What we mean in a song,
Some people don't know.

Some people don't know
That we weren't born to cry,
Some people don't know
That the sun in the sky
Was made for an earth
Where the roots do not die,
Some people don't know;

And they don't even know
When they shout what we dream
They're misreading our thoughts
That have no mighty theme,
We just want to grow
Through a season of green,
Some people don't know.

I. R. ORTON
born 1926

A Piper

A piper in the street today
Set up, and tuned, and started to play,
And away, away, away on the tide
Of his music we started; on every side
Doors and windows were opened wide,
And men left down their work and came,
And women with petticoats coloured like flame.
And little bare feet that were blue with cold,
Went dancing back to the age of gold,
And all the world went gay, went gay,
For half an hour in the street today.

SEUMAS O'SULLIVAN
1879 – 1958

Jazz Fantasia

Drum on your drums, batter on your banjos, sob on the
long cool winding saxophones. Go to it, O jazzmen.

Sling your knuckles on the bottoms of the happy tin
pans, let your trombones ooze, and go husha-husha-
hush with the slippery sandpaper.

Moan like an autumn wind high in the lonesome treetops, moan soft like you wanted somebody terrible,
cry like a racing car slipping away from a motorcycle-
cop, bang-bang! you jazzmen, bang altogether drums,
traps, banjos, horns, tin cans – make two people
fight on the top of a stairway and scratch each other's
eyes in a clinch tumbling down the stairs.

Can the rough stuff . . . Now a Mississippi steamboat
pushes up the night river with a hoo-hoo-hoo-oo . . .
and the green lanterns calling to the high soft stars . . .
a red moon rides on the humps of the low river
hills . . . Go to it, O jazzmen.

CARL SANDBURG
1878 – 1967

Saturday Night

Play it once.
O, play it some more.
Charlie is a gambler
An' Sadie is a whore
   A glass o' whiskey
   An' a glass o' gin:
   Strut, Mr Charlie,
   Till de dawn comes in.
Pawn yo' gold watch
An' diamond ring.
Git a quart o' licker.
Let's shake dat thing!
   Skee-de-dad! De-dad!
   Doo-doo-doo!
   Won't be nothin' left
   When de worms git through.
   An' you's a long time
   Dead
   When you is
   Dead, too.
So beat dat drum, boy!
Shout dat song:
Shake 'em up an' shake 'em up
All night long.
   Hey! Hey!
   Ho . . . Hum!
   Do it, Mr Charlie,
   Till de red dawn come.

LANGSTON HUGHES
born 1902

The Weary Blues

Droning a drowsy syncopated tune
Rocking back and forth to a mellow croon,
　I heard a Negro play.
Down on Lenox Avenue the other night
By the pale dull pallor of an old gas light
　He did a lazy sway . . .
　He did a lazy sway . . .
To the tune o' those Weary Blues.
With his ebony hands on each ivory key
He made that poor piano moan with melody.
　O Blues!
Swaying to and fro on his rickety stool
He played that sad raggy tune like a musical fool.
　Sweet Blues!
Coming from a black man's soul.
　O Blues!
In a deep song voice with a melancholy tone
I heard that Negro sing, that old piano moan –
　'Ain't got nobody in all this world,
　Ain't got nobody but ma self.
　I's gwine to quit ma frownin'
　And put ma troubles on the shelf.'
Thump, thump, thump, went his foot on the floor.
He played a few chords then he sang some more –
　'I got the Weary Blues
　And I can't be satisfied.
　Got the Weary Blues
　And can't be satisfied –
　I ain't happy no mo'
　And I wish that I had died.'
And far into the night he crooned that tune.
The stars went out and so did the moon.
The singer stopped playing and went to bed
While the Weary Blues echoed through his head.
He slept like a rock or a man that's dead.

LANGSTON HUGHES
born 1902

Yellow Crane Tower

To the Melody of P'u Sa Man   Summer, 1927

Broad, broad
   through the country
   flow the nine tributaries.
Deep, deep
   from north to south
   cuts a line.
Blurred in the blue haze
   of the rain and mist
The Snake and Tortoise Hills
   tower above the water.

The yellow crane
   has departed.
   Who knows where it has gone?
Only this resting-place
   for travellers remains.
In wine I drink
   a pledge to the surging torrent.
The tide of my heart
   rises as high as the waves.

MAO TSE-TUNG
born 1893
Translated from the Chinese
by Jerome Ch'en and Michael Bullock

Scarborough Fair

Where are you going? To Scarborough Fair?
Parsley, sage, rosemary and thyme,
Remember me to a bonny lass there,
For once she was a true lover of mine.

Tell her to make me a cambric shirt,
Parsley, sage, rosemary and thyme,
Without any needle or thread work'd in it,
And she shall be a true lover of mine.

Tell her to wash it in yonder well,
Parsley, sage, rosemary and thyme,
Where water ne'er sprung nor a drop of rain fell,
And she shall be a true lover of mine.

Tell her to plough me an acre of land,
Parsley, sage, rosemary and thyme,
Between the sea and the salt sea strand,
And she shall be a true lover of mine.

Tell her to plough it with one ram's horn,
Parsley, sage, rosemary and thyme,
And sow it all over with one peppercorn,
And she shall be a true lover of mine.

Tell her to reap it with a sickle of leather,
Parsley, sage, rosemary and thyme,
And tie it all up with a tom tit's feather,
And she shall be a true lover of mine.

Tell her to gather it all in a sack,
Parsley, sage, rosemary and thyme,
And carry it home on a butterfly's back,
And then she shall be a true lover of mine.

ANON.

Ariel's Song
From *The Tempest*

Come unto these yellow sands,
  And then take hands:
Curtsied when you have, and kiss'd
  The wild waves whist,
 Foot it featly here and there;
And, sweet sprites, the burden bear.
  Hark, hark!
    Bow, wow,
  The watch-dogs bark,
    Bow, wow,
  Hark, hark! I hear
The strain of strutting Chanticleer
Cry, Cock-a-diddle-dow.

WILLIAM SHAKESPEARE
1564 – 1616

Full Fathom Five Thy Father Lies
From *The Tempest*

Full fathom five thy father lies;
  Of his bones are coral made;
Those are pearls that were his eyes:
  Nothing of him that doth fade,
But doth suffer a sea-change
Into something rich and strange.
Sea-nymphs hourly ring his knell:
        Ding-dong!
  Hark! now I hear them,
      Ding-dong, bell!

WILLIAM SHAKESPEARE
1564 – 1616

A New Song on the Birth of the Prince of Wales

Who was born on Tuesday, 9th November 1841

There's a pretty fuss and bother both in country and in town,
Since we have got a present, and an heir unto the Crown,
A little Prince of Wales so charming and so sly,
And the ladies shout with wonder, What a pretty little boy!

He must have a little musket, a trumpet and a kite,
A little penny rattle, and silver sword so bright,
A little cap and feather with scarlet coat so smart,
And a pretty little hobby horse to ride about the park.

Prince Albert he will often take the young Prince on his lap,
And fondle him so lovingly while he stirs about the pap,
He will pin on his flannel before he takes his nap,
Then dress him out so stylish with his little clouts and cap.

He must have a dandy suit to strut about the town,
John Bull must rake together six or seven thousand pound,
You'd laugh to see his daddy, at night he homewards runs,
With some peppermint or lollipops, sweet cakes and sugar
    plums.

He will want a little fiddle, and a little German flute,
A little pair of stockings and a pretty pair of boots,
With a handsome pair of spurs, and a golden headed cane,
And a stick of barley sugar, as long as Drury Lane.

An old maid ran through the palace, which did the nobs
    surprize,
Bawling out, he's got his daddy's mouth, his mammy's nose and
    eyes,
He will be as like his daddy as a frigate to a ship,
If he'd only got mustachios upon his upper lip.

Now to get these little niceties the taxes must be rose,
For the little Prince of Wales wants so many suits of clothes,
So they must tax the frying pan, the windows and the doors,
The bedsteads and the tables, kitchen pokers, and the floors.

ANON.

Japanese Cradle Song

Grass for my pillow,
The night is green,
Stars for my window
And stones for my dream.

Grass for my pillow,
The night is green,
Sand for my sorrow
And snow for my screen.

Grass for my pillow,
The day is dead,
Dust for my shadow
And earth for my bed.

Grass for my pillow,
The day is dead,
Clouds for my cover
And rain for my shed.

Grass for my pillow,
Black is the wave,
Grass for my pillow,
Grass for a grave.

JAMES KIRKUP
born 1923

131

London Bells

Gay go up, and gay go down,
To ring the bells of London town.

Bull's eyes and targets,
Say the bells of St Marg'ret's.

Brickbats and tiles,
Say the bells of St Giles'.

Halfpence and farthings
Say the bells of St Martin's.

Oranges and lemons,
Say the bells of St Clement's.

Pancakes and fritters,
Say the bells of St Peter's.

Two sticks and an apple,
Say the bells at Whitechapel.

Old Father Baldpate,
Say the slow bells at Aldgate.

Maids in white aprons,
Say the bells of St Cath'rine's.

Pokers and tongs,
Say the bells at St John's.

Kettles and pans,
Say the bells at St Ann's.

You owe me ten shillings,
Say the bells at St Helen's.

When will you pay me?
Say the bells at Old Bailey.

When I grow rich,
Say the bells at Fleetditch.

When will that be?
Say the bells at Stepney.

I am sure I don't know,
Says the great bell at Bow.

When I am old,
Say the bells at St Paul's.

Here comes a candle to light you to bed,
And here comes a chopper to chop off your head.

ANON.

From **Gwalia Deserta**

O what can you give me?
Say the sad bells of Rhymney.

Is there hope for the future?
Cry the brown bells of Merthyr.

Who made the mineowner?
Say the black bells of Rhondda.

And who robbed the miner?
Cry the grim bells of Blaina.

They will plunder willy-nilly,
Say the bells of Caerphilly.

They have fangs, they have teeth!
Shout the loud bells of Neath.

To the south, things are sullen,
Say the pink bells of Brecon.

Even God is uneasy,
Say the moist bells of Swansea.

Put the vandals in court!
Cry the bells of Newport.

All would be well if–if–if–
Say the green bells of Cardiff.

Why so worried, sisters, why?
Sing the silver bells of Wye.

IDRIS DAVIES
born 1905

Perpetuum Mobile : The Broken Record
Theme and Variations

I did not know
What love might be
Until you gave
Your hand to me.

I did not know
Not know not know
What love might be might be,
Not wishing I might understand
The wonders found within the land
Of grief and lost within the grave,
Until until you gave you gave
Your hand to me, your hand
To me, you gave your hand to me.

For in your hand
I felt your heart,
And found I held
The rose of thought.

For in your hand
Your hand your hand
I felt I felt your heart,
Your breath that goes and comes and goes,
And slows and quickens, quickens, slows,
Quick-quickens, willingly compelled,
And found and found I held I held
The rose of thought, the rose
Of thought, I held the rose of thought.

The thought was sweet,
The rose was wild,
And love was love
To man and child.

The thought was sweet
Was sweet was sweet,
The rose was wild was wild,
A bird sang and the spring began
The song that cannot cannot can
Be sung, and makes our living live,
That love is love is love is love
Is love to child and man
And child is love to man and child.

The thought is sweet.
The rose is wild,
And love is love
To man and child.

JAMES KIRKUP
born 1923

Song

The feathers of the willow
Are half of them grown yellow
   Above the swelling stream;
And ragged are the bushes,
And rusty now the rushes,
   And wild the clouded gleam.

The thistle now is older,
His stalk begins to moulder,
   His head is white as snow;
The branches all are barer,
The linnet's song is rarer,
   The robin pipeth now.

RICHARD WATSON DIXON
1737 – 1811

Chorus from **Atalanta**

Before the beginning of years
   There came to the making of man
Time, with a gift of tears;
   Grief, with a glass that ran;
Pleasure, with pain for leaven;
   Summer, with flowers that fell;
Remembrance fallen from heaven,
   And madness risen from hell;
Strength without hands to smite;
   Love that endures for a breath;
Night, the shadow of light,
   And life, the shadow of death.
And the high gods took in hand
   Fire, and the falling of tears,
And a measure of sliding sand
   From under the feet of the years;
And froth and drift of the sea;
   And dust of the labouring earth;
And bodies of things to be
   In the houses of death and of birth;
And wrought with weeping and laughter,
   And fashion'd with loathing and love,
With life before and after
   And death beneath and above,
For a day and a night and a morrow,
   That his strength might endure for a span
With travail and heavy sorrow,
   The holy spirit of man.

From the winds of the north and the south
   They gather'd as unto strife;
They breathed upon his mouth,
   They filled his body with life;
Eyesight and speech they wrought
   For the veils of the soul therein,
A time for labour and thought,
   A time to serve and to sin;

They gave him light in his ways,
   And love, and a space for delight,
And beauty and length of days,
   And night, and sleep in the night.
His speech is a burning fire;
   With his lips he travaileth;
In his heart is a blind desire,
   In his eyes foreknowledge of death;
He weaves, and is clothed with derision;
   Sows, and he shall not reap;
His life is a watch or a vision
   Between a sleep and a sleep.

ALGERNON CHARLES SWINBURNE
1837 – 1909

Chorus from **Prometheus Unbound**

My soul is an enchanted boat,
   Which, like a sleeping swan, doth float
Upon the silver waves of thy sweet singing;
   And thine doth like an angel sit
   Beside the helm conducting it,
Whilst all the winds with melody are ringing.
   It seems to float ever, for ever,
   Upon that many-winding river,
   Between mountains, woods, abysses,
   A paradise of wildernesses!
Till, like one in slumber bound,
Borne to the ocean, I float down, around,
Into a sea profound, of ever-spreading sound.

PERCY BYSSHE SHELLEY
1792 – 1822

Song from **The Underwood**

Have you seene but a bright Lillie grow,
   Before rude hands have touch'd it?
Have you mark'd but the fall of the snow
   Before the soyle hath smutched it?
Have you felt the wooll o' the Bever?
      Or Swans Downe ever?
Or have smelt o' the bud o' the Brier?
      Or the Nard i' the fire?
   Or have tasted the bag o' the Bee?
O so white! O so soft! O so sweet is she!

BEN JONSON
1573 – 1637

Dirge in Woods

A wind sways the pines,
   And below
Not a breath of wild air;
Still as the mosses that glow
On the flooring and over the lines
Of the roots here and there.
The pine-tree drops its dead;
They are quiet, as under the sea.
Overhead, overhead
Rushes life in a race,
As the clouds the clouds chase;
     And we go,
And we drop like the fruits of the tree,
     Even we,
     Even so.

GEORGE MEREDITH
1828 – 1909

Fun and games

Pooh!

Pretty Miss Apathy
Sat on a sofa
Dangling her legs,
And with nothing to do.
She looked at the picture of
Old Queen Victoria,
The rug from far Persia –
An exquisite blue;
She looked at the switch
That evokes e-
Lectricity,
At the coals of an age
B.C. millions and two,
When the trees were like ferns
And the reptiles all flew;
She looked at the cat
In dream on the hearthrug,
At the sky at the window,
The clouds in it, too,
Gilt with marvellous light
From the west burning through;
And the one silly word
In her desolate noddle
As she dangled her legs,
Having nothing to do,
Was not, as you'd guess,
Of dumfoundered felicity,
But contained just four letters,
And these pronounced 'Pooh!'

WALTER DE LA MARE
1873 – 1956

A Nocturnal Sketch

Even is come; and from the dark Park, hark,
The signal of the setting sun – one gun!
And six is sounding from the chime, prime time
To go and see the Drury-Lane Dane slain, –
Or hear Othello's jealous doubt spout out, –
Or Macbeth raving at that shade-made blade,
Denying to his frantic clutch much touch; –
Or else to see Ducrow with wide stride ride
Four horses as no other man can span;
Or in the small Olympic Pit, sit split
Laughing at Liston, while you quiz his phiz.

Anon Night comes, and with her wings brings things
Such as, with his poetic tongue, Young sung;
The gas up-blazes with its bright white light,
And paralytic watchmen prowl, howl, growl,
About the streets and take up Pall-Mall Sal,
Who, hasting to her nightly jobs, robs fobs.

Now thieves to enter for your cash, smash, crash,
Past drowsy Charley in a deep sleep, creep,
But frightened by Policeman B3, flee,
And while they're going, whisper low, 'No go!'

Now puss, while folks are in their beds, treads leads
And sleepers waking, grumble – 'Drat that cat!'
Who in the gutter caterwauls, squalls, mauls
Some feline foe, and screams in shrill ill-will.

Now Bulls of Bashan, of a prize size, rise
In childish dreams, and with a roar gore poor
Georgy, or Charley, or Billy, willy-nilly; –
But Nursemaid, in a nightmare rest, chest-press'd,
Dreameth of one of her old flames, James Games,
And that she hears – what faith is man's! – Ann's banns
And his, from Reverend Mr Rice, twice, thrice:
White ribbons flourish, and a stout shout out,
That upward goes, shows Rose knows those bows' woes!

THOMAS HOOD
1799 – 1845

I Remember Arnold

I remember Kakky Hargreaves
As if 'twer Yestermorn'
Kakky, Kakky Hargreaves
Son of Mr Vaughan.

He used to be so grundie
On him little bike
Riding on a Sundie
Funny little tyke

Yes, I remember Kathy Hairbream
As if 'twer yesterday
Katthy, Kathy Hairbream
Son of Mr May

Arriving at the station
Always dead on time
For his destination
Now He's dead on line
(meaning he's been got by a train or something)

And so we growt and bumply
Till the end of time,
Humpty dumpty bumply
Son of Harry Lime.

Bumbleydy Hubledy Humbley
Bumdley Tum. (Thank you)

JOHN LENNON
born 1940

Hunter Trials

It's awf'lly bad luck on Diana,
   Her ponies have swallowed their bits;
She fished down their throats with a spanner
   And frightened them all into fits.

So now she's attempting to borrow.
   Do lend her some bits, Mummy, *do*;
I'll lend her my own for tomorrow,
   But today *I*'ll be wanting them too.

Just look at Prunella on Guzzle,
   The wizardest pony on earth;
Why doesn't she slacken his muzzle
   And tighten the breech in his girth?

I say, Mummy, there's Mrs Geyser
   And doesn't she look pretty sick?
I bet it's because Mona Lisa
   Was hit on the hock with a brick.

Miss Blewitt says Monica threw it,
   But Monica says it was Joan,
And Joan's very thick with Miss Blewitt,
   So Monica's sulking alone.

And Margaret failed in her paces,
   Her withers got tied in a noose,
So her coronets caught in the traces
   And now all her fetlocks are loose.

Oh, it's me now. I'm terribly nervous.
I wonder if Smudges will shy.
She's practically certain to swerve as
Her Pelham is over one eye.

*   *   *

Oh wasn't it naughty of Smudges?
Oh, Mummy, I'm sick with disgust.
She threw me in front of the Judges,
And my silly old collarbone's bust.

JOHN BETJEMAN
born 1906

I Wandered

On balmy seas and pernie schooners
On strivers and warming things
In a peanut coalshed clad
I wandered happy as a jew
To meet good Doris King.

Past grisby trees and hulky builds
Past ratters and bradder sheep
In a resus baby stooped
I wandered hairy as a dog
To get a goobites sleep.

Down hovey lanes and stoney claves
Down ricketts and sticklys myth
In a fatty hebrew gurth
I wandered humply as a sock
To meet bad Bernie Smith.

JOHN LENNON
born 1940

K   145

anyone lived in a pretty how town

anyone lived in a pretty how town
(with up so floating many bells down)
spring summer autumn winter
he sang his didn't he danced his did.

Women and men(both little and small)
cared for anyone not at all
they sowed their isn't they reaped their same
sun moon stars rain

children guessed(but only a few
and down they forgot as up they grew
autumn winter spring summer)
that no one loved him more by more

when by now and tree by leaf
she laughed his joy she cried his grief
bird by snow and stir by still
anyone's any was all to her

someones married their everyones
laughed their cryings and did their dance
(sleep wake hope and then)they
said their nevers they slept their dream

stars rain sun moon
(and only the snow can begin to explain
how children are apt to forget to remember
with up so floating many bells down)

one day anyone died i guess
(and no-one stooped to kiss his face)
busy folk buried them side by side
little by little and was by was

all by all and deep by deep
and more by more they dream their sleep
no-one and anyone earth by april
wish by spirit and if by yes.

Women and men(both dong and ding)
summer autumn winter spring
reaped their sowing and went their came
sun moon stars rain

E. E. CUMMINGS
1894 – 1962

The Latest Decalogue

Thou shalt have one God only; who
Would be at the expense of two?

No graven images may be
Worshipp'd, except the currency:

Swear not at all; for, for thy curse
Thine enemy is none the worse:

At church on Sunday to attend
Will serve to keep the world thy friend:

Honour thy parents; that is, all
From whom advancement may befall:

Thou shalt not kill; but need'st not strive
Officiously to keep alive:

Do not adultery commit;
Advantage rarely comes of it:

Thou shalt not steal; an empty feat,
When 'tis so lucrative to cheat:

Bear not false witness; let the lie
Have time on its own wings to fly:

Thou shalt not covet, but tradition
Approves all forms of competition.

ARTHUR HUGH CLOUGH
1819 – 1861

Inhuman Henry *or* Cruelty to Fabulous Animals

Oh would you know why Henry sleeps,
And why his mourning Mother weeps,
And why his weeping Mother mourns?
He was unkind to unicorns.

No unicorn, with Henry's leave,
Could dance upon the lawn at eve,
Or gore the gardener's boy in spring
Or do the very slightest thing.

No unicorn could safely roar,
And dash its nose against the door,
Nor sit in peace upon the mat
To eat the dog, or drink the cat.

Henry would never in the least
Encourage the heraldic beast:
If there were unicorns about
He went and let the lion out.

The lion, leaping from its chain
And glaring through its tangled mane,
Would stand on end and bark and bound
And bite what unicorns it found.

And when the lion bit a lot
Was Henry sorry? He was not.
What did his jumps betoken? Joy.
He was a bloody-minded boy.

The Unicorn is not a Goose,
And when they saw the lion loose,
They grew increasingly aware
That they had better not be there.

And oh, the unicorn is fleet
And spurns the earth with all its feet.
The lion had to snap and snatch
At tips of tails it could not catch.

Returning home in temper bad,
It met the sanguinary lad,
And clasping Henry with its claws
It took his legs between its jaws

'Down, lion, down!' said Henry, 'cease!
My legs immediately release.'
His formidable feline pet
Made no reply, but only ate.

The last words that were ever said
By Henry's disappearing head,
In accents of indignant scorn,
Were 'I am not a unicorn.'

And now you know why Henry sleeps,
And why his Mother mourns and weeps,
And why she also weeps and mourns;
So now be nice to unicorns.

A. E. HOUSMAN
1859 – 1936

Honesty at a Fire

What a calamity! What dreadful loss!
  How sad 'twould be if anyone were dead.
Still no fire engine! Look, it leaps across!
  O how I hope this lovely fire will spread!

J. C. SQUIRE
1884 – 1958

An Epicure, Dining at Crewe

An epicure, dining at Crewe,
Found a large mouse in his stew.
  Said the waiter, 'Don't shout
  And wave it about,
Or the rest will be wanting one, too!'

ANON.

Literary Dinner

Come here, said my hostess, her face making room
for one of those pink introductory smiles
that link, like a valley of fruit trees in bloom,
the slopes of two names.
I want you, she murmured, to eat Dr James.

I was hungry. The Doctor looked good. He had read
the great book of the week, and had liked it, he said,
because it was powerful. So I was brought
a generous helping. His mauve-bosomed wife
kept showing me, very politely, I thought,
the tenderest bits with the point of her knife.
I ate – and in Egypt the sunsets were swell;
The Russians were doing remarkably well;
Had I met a Prince Poprinsky, whom he had known
in Caparabella, or was it Mentone?
They had travelled extensively, he and his wife;
her hobby was People, his hobby was Life.
All was good and well cooked, but the tastiest part
was his nut-flavoured, crisp cerebellum. The heart
resembled a shiny brown date,
and I stowed all the studs on the edge of my plate.

VLADIMIR NABOKOV
born 1899

Christmastide

Saint John Baptist

The last and greatest Herald of Heaven's King,
Girt with rough skins, hies to the deserts wild,
Among that savage brood the woods forth bring,
Which he than man more harmless found, and mild.
His food was locusts, and what there doth spring
With honey that from virgin hives distill'd;
Parch'd body, hollow eyes, some uncouth thing
Made him appear, long since from earth exiled.
There burst he forth: 'All ye whose hopes rely
On God, with me amidst these deserts mourn;
Repent, repent, and from old errors turn!'
– Who listen'd to his voice, obey'd his cry?
Only the echoes, which he made relent,
Rung from their flinty caves, 'Repent! Repent!'

WILLIAM DRUMMOND, OF HAWTHORNDEN
1585 – 1649

The Shepherd's Tale

Woman, you'll never credit what
    My two eyes saw this night . . .
But first of all we'll have a drop,
    It's freezing now, all right.

It was the queerest going-on
    That I did e'er behold:
A holy child out in the barn,
    A baby all in gold.

Now let's get started on the soup,
    And let me tell it you,
For though there's not a thing made up,
    It still seems hardly true.

There he was laid upon the straw,
    Will you dish up the stew?
The ass did bray, the hens did craw,
    I'll have some cabbage too.

First there was a king from Prussia,
    At least that's how he looked,
Then there was the king of Russia.
    This stew's been overcooked.

There they were kneeling on the ground.
    Come, have a bite to eat.
First I just stared and stood around.
    Have just a taste of meat!

Well, one of them he ups and says
    A long speech – kind of funny.
Here, what about that last new cheese,
    Is it still runny?

The little'un, wise as wise could be,
　　Just didn't care for that.
But he was pleased as punch with me
　　When I took off me hat.

I took his little fists in mine,
　　In front of all those nobs.
Fetch us a jug of our best wine
　　My dear, we'll wet our gobs.

That very instant, as if I'd
　　Had a good swig of drink,
I felt a great warm joy inside,
　　But why, I cannot think.

Ah, this wine's the stuff, by Mary!
　　When he's grown up a bit,
That little fellow, just you see,
　　He shall have some of it!

We might have all been knelt there yet,
　　Put a Yule log on the fire,
But suddenly he starts to fret –
　　He'd begun to tire.

Then 'Sirs,' his mother she did say,
　　'It grieves me to remind
You that it's time to go away
　　When you have been so kind.

'But see, how sleepy he's become,
　　He's crying, let him rest.
You all know how to find our home
　　Each one's a welcome guest.'

And so in silence we went out,
   But the funniest thing –
Those three fine kings, so rich and stout,
   Did wish me good-morning!

You see, love, that's how it began.
   The God born on the earth
This night's no ordinary one.
   Let's celebrate his birth!

RAOUL PONCHON
1848 – 1937
*Translated from the French
by James Kirkup*

Preparations

From a Ms. at Christ Church, Oxford

Yet if His Majesty, our sovereign lord,
Should of his own accord
Friendly himself invite,
And say 'I'll be your guest tomorrow night,'
How should we stir ourselves, call and command
All hands to work! 'Let no man idle stand!

'Set me fine Spanish tables in the hall;
See they be fitted all;
Let there be room to eat
And order taken that there want no meat.
See every sconce and candlestick made bright,
That without tapers they may give a light.

'Look to the presence: are the carpets spread,
The dazie* o'er the head,
The cushions in the chairs,

And all the candles lighted on the stairs?
Perfume the chambers, and in any case
Let each man give attendance in his place!'

Thus, if a king were coming, would we do;
And 'twere good reason too;
For 'tis a duteous thing
To show all honour to an earthly king,
And, after all our travail and our cost,
So he be pleased, to think no labour lost.

But at the coming of the King of Heaven
All's set at six and seven;
We wallow in our sin,
Christ cannot find a chamber in the inn.
We entertain Him always like a stranger,
And, as at first, still lodge Him in the manger.

* *dazie:* a canopy over the throne

ANON.

Picture of the Nativity in
the Church of Krena in Chios

– Tell me, can this unsuspecting infant, staring
At the steep green sky, be 'He, who trampled upon Death'?
Everything round him is so poor and so untrue,
The brown ponies like shabby toys, the shepherds stilted
On their crooks, the Magi wooden kings that dare not bend,
Even the angels, village angels – they could never
Reach the sky again with those flat, clumsy wings.

– Silently, unawares and unbelievably come all
Great things: the inroad of great love, the mist of death.

CONSTANTINE TRYPANIS
born 1909

From   A Christmas Childhood
Part II

My father played the melodion
Outside at our gate;
There were stars in the morning east
And they danced to his music.

Across the wild bogs his melodion called
To Lennons and Callans.
As I pulled on my trousers in a hurry
I knew some strange thing had happened.

Outside in the cow-house my mother
Made the music of milking;
The light of her stable-lamp was a star
And the frost of Bethlehem made it twinkle.

A water-hen screeched in the bog,
Mass-going feet
Crunched the wafer-ice on the pot-holes,
Somebody wistfully twisted the bellows wheel.

My child poet picked out the letters
On the grey stone,
In silver the wonder of a Christmas townland,
The winking glitter of a frosty dawn.

Cassiopeia was over
Cassidy's hanging hill,
I looked and three whin bushes rode across
The horizon – the Three Wise Kings.

An old man passing said:
'Can't he make it talk' –
The melodion. I hid in the doorway
And tightened the belt of my box-pleated coat.

I nicked six nicks on the door-post
With my penknife's big blade –
There was a little one for cutting tobacco.
And I was six Christmases of age.

My father played the melodion,
My mother milked the cows,
And I had a prayer like a white rose pinned
On the Virgin Mary's blouse.

PATRICK KAVANAGH
1905 – 1967

Carol

There was a Boy bedded in bracken,
    Like to a sleeping snake all curled he lay;
        On his thin navel turned this spinning sphere,
            Each feeble finger fetched seven suns away.
            He was not dropped in good-for-lambing weather,
            He took no suck when shook buds sing together,
            But he is come in cold-as-workhouse weather,
                Poor as a Salford child.

JOHN SHORT
born 1911

The Burning Babe

As I in hoary winter's night
   Stood shivering in the snow,
Surprised I was with sudden heat
   Which made my heart to glow;
And lifting up a fearful eye
   To view what fire was near,
A pretty babe all burning bright
   Did in the air appear;
Who, scorchèd with excessive heat,
   Such floods of tears did shed,
As though His floods should quench His flames,
   Which with His tears were bred:
'Alas!' quoth He, 'but newly born
   In fiery heats I fry,
Yet none approach to warm their hearts
   Or feel my fire but I!

'My faultless breast the furnace is;
   The fuel, wounding thorns;
Love is the fire, and sighs the smoke;
   The ashes, shames and scorns;
The fuel Justice layeth on,
   And Mercy blows the coals,
The metal in this furnace wrought
   Are men's defilèd souls:
For which, as now on fire I am
   To work them to their good,
So I will melt into a bath,
   To wash them in my blood.'
With this He vanish'd out of sight
   And swiftly shrunk away,
And straight I callèd unto mind
   That it was Christmas Day.

ROBERT SOUTHWELL
1561 ? – 1595

From In Memoriam

Ring out, wild bells, to the wild sky,
  The flying cloud, the frosty light:
  The year is dying in the night;
Ring out, wild bells, and let him die.

Ring out the old, ring in the new,
  Ring, happy bells, across the snow:
  The year is going, let him go;
Ring out the false, ring in the true.

Ring out the grief that saps the mind,
  For those that here we see no more;
  Ring out the feud of rich and poor,
Ring in redress to all mankind.

Ring out a slowly dying cause,
  And ancient forms of party strife;
  Ring in the nobler modes of life,
With sweeter manners, purer laws.

Ring out the want, the care, the sin,
  The faithless coldness of the times;
  Ring out, ring out my mournful rhymes,
But ring the fuller minstrel in.

Ring out false pride in place and blood,
  The civic slander and the spite;
  Ring in the love of truth and right,
Ring in the common love of good.

Ring out old shapes of foul disease;
  Ring out the narrowing lust of gold;
  Ring out the thousand wars of old,
Ring in the thousand years of peace.

Ring in the valiant man and free,
  The larger heart, the kindlier hand;
  Ring out the darkness of the land,
Ring in the Christ that is to be.

ALFRED, LORD TENNYSON
1809 – 1892

Twelfth Night

The feast has ended; now outside the door
Stands the stripped Christmas tree without a star,
Bare as the barren branch that lightning struck;
And paper garlands from the public house
Lie in the gutter now, without a use.

The sacred child is lost in streets unnamed,
And from the silent sky the glory sinks,
Burnt out upon the darkness and the cold,
While, packed away with fragile decorations,
The vision of a birth, like these, must wait.

The world cannot maintain, it makes quite clear,
Angels and praying shepherds all the year.

I. R. ORTON
born 1926

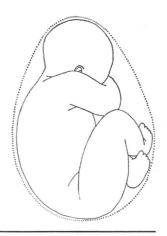

O world! O life! O time!

A Lament

O world! O life! O time!
On whose last steps I climb,
  Trembling at that where I had stood before;
When will return the glory of your prime?
  No more – Oh, never more!

Out of the day and night
A joy has taken flight;
  Fresh spring, and summer, and winter hoar
Move my faint heart with grief, but with delight
  No more – Oh, never more!

PERCY BYSSHE SHELLEY
1792 – 1822

The Life of Man

A blast of wind, a momentary breath,
A watery bubble symbolized with air,
A sun-blown rose, but for a season fair,
A ghostly glance, a skeleton of death;
A morning dew, pearling the grass beneath,
Whose moisture sun's appearance doth impair;
A lightning glimpse, a muse of thought and care,
A planet's shot, a shade which followeth,
A voice which vanisheth so soon as heard,
The thriftless heir of time, a rolling wave,
A show, no more in action than regard,
A mass of dust, world's momentary slave,
  Is man, in state of our old Adam made,
  Soon born to die, soon flourishing to fade.

BARNABE BARNES
1569 ? – 1609

The World's a Bubble

The world's a bubble, and the life of man
   Less than a span,
In his conception wretched, from the womb,
   So to the tomb;
Curst from the cradle, and brought up to years,
   With cares and fears.
Who then to frail mortality shall trust,
But limns on water, or but writes in dust.

Yet since with sorrow here we live oppressed,
   What life is best?
Courts are but only superficial schools
   To dandle fools.
The rural parts are turned into a den
   Of savage men.
And where's a city from all vice so free,
But may be termed the worst of all the three?

Domestic cares afflict the husband's bed,
   Or pains his head.
Those that live single take it for a curse,
   Or do things worse.
Some would have children; those that have them none,
   Or wish them gone.
What is it then to have or have no wife,
But single thraldom, or a double strife?

Our own affections still at home to please
   Is a disease;
To cross the sea to any foreign soil,
   Perils and toil.
Wars with their noise affright us; when they cease,
   W'are worse in peace.
What then remains, but that we still should cry,
Not to be born, or being born to die?

SIR FRANCIS BACON
1561 – 1626

Has Sorrow Thy Young Days Shaded?

Has sorrow thy young days shaded,
  As clouds o'er the morning fleet?
Too fast have those young days faded,
  That, even in sorrow, were sweet?
Does Time with his cold wing wither
  Each feeling that once was dear?
Then, child of misfortune, come hither,
  I'll weep with thee, tear for tear.

Has Hope, like the bird in the story,
  That flitted from tree to tree
With the talisman's glittering glory –
  Has Hope been that bird to thee?
On branch after branch alighting,
  The gem did she still display,
And, when nearest and most inviting,
  Then waft the fair gem away?

If thus the young hours have fleeted,
  When sorrow itself looked bright;
If thus the fair hope hath cheated,
  That led thee along so light;
If thus the cold world now wither
  Each feeling that once was dear; –
Come, child of misfortune, come hither,
  I'll weep with thee, tear for tear.

THOMAS MOORE
1779 – 1852

The Laws of God

The laws of God, the laws of man,
He may keep that will and can;
Not I: let God and man decree
Laws for themselves and not for me;
And if my ways are not as theirs
Let them mind their own affairs.
Their deeds I judge and much condemn,
Yet when did I make laws for them?
Please yourselves, say I, and they
Need only look the other way.
But no, they will not; they must still
Wrest their neighbour to their will,
And make me dance as they desire
With jail and gallows and hell-fire.
And how am I to face the odds
Of man's bedevilment and God's?
I, a stranger and afraid
In a world I never made.
They will be master, right or wrong;
Though both are foolish, both are strong.
And since, my soul, we cannot fly
To Saturn nor to Mercury,
Keep we must, if keep we can,
These foreign laws of God and man.

A. E. HOUSMAN
1859 – 1936

Youth and Age

There's not a joy the world can give like that it takes away,
When the glow of early thought declines in feeling's dull decay;
'Tis not on youth's smooth cheek the blush alone, which fades
so fast,
But the tender bloom of heart is gone, ere youth itself be past.

Then the few whose spirits float above the wreck of happiness
Are driven o'er the shoals of guilt, or ocean of excess:
The magnet of their course is gone, or only points in vain
The shore to which their shiver'd sail shall never stretch again.

Then the mortal coldness of the soul like death itself comes
down;
It cannot feel for others' woes, it dare not dream its own;
That heavy chill has frozen o'er the fountain of our tears,
And though the eye may sparkle still, 'tis where the ice appears.

Though wit may flash from fluent lips, and mirth distract the
breast,
Through midnight hours that yield no more their former hope
of rest;
'Tis but as ivy-leaves around the ruin'd turret wreathe,
All green and wildly fresh without, but worn and grey beneath.

Oh could I feel as I have felt, – or be what I have been,
Or weep as I could once have wept o'er many a vanish'd
scene;
As springs in deserts found seem sweet, all brackish though
they be,
So, midst the wither'd waste of life, those tears would flow to
me.

GEORGE GORDON, LORD BYRON
1788 – 1824

Stanzas Written in Dejection, near Naples

The sun is warm, the sky is clear,
　The waves are dancing fast and bright,
Blue isles and snowy mountains wear
　　The purple noon's transparent might,
　　The breath of the moist earth is light,
Around its unexpanded buds;
　　Like many a voice of one delight,
The winds, the birds, the ocean-floods,
The City's voice itself, is soft like Solitude's.

I see the Deep's untrampled floor
　With green and purple seaweeds strown;
I see the waves upon the shore,
　　Like light dissolved in star-showers, thrown:
　　I sit upon the sands alone, –
The lightning of the noontide ocean
　　Is flashing round me, and a tone
Arises from its measured motion,
How sweet! did any heart now share in my emotion.

Alas! I have nor hope nor health,
　Nor peace within nor calm around,
Nor that content surpassing wealth
　　The sage in meditation found,
　　And walked with inward glory crowned –
Nor fame, nor power, nor love, nor leisure.
　　Others I see whom these surround –
Smiling they live, and call life pleasure; –
To me that cup has been dealt in another measure.

Yet now despair itself is mild,
　Even as the winds and waters are;
I could lie down like a tired child,
　　And weep away the life of care
　　Which I have borne and yet must bear,
Till death like sleep might steal on me,
　　And I might feel in the warm air
My cheek grow cold, and hear the sea
Breathe o'er my dying brain its last monotony.

Some might lament that I were cold,
　　As I, when this sweet day is gone,
Which my lost heart, too soon grown old,
　　Insults with this untimely moan;
　　They might lament – for I am one
Whom men love not, – and yet regret,
　　Unlike this day, which, when the sun
　　Shall on its stainless glory set,
Will linger, though enjoyed, like joy in memory yet.

PERCY BYSSHE SHELLEY
1792 – 1822

O ! Why Was I Born with a Different Face ?

O! why was I born with a different face?
Why was I not born like the rest of my race?
When I look, each one starts; when I speak, I offend;
Then I'm silent and passive, and lose every friend.

Then my verse I dishonour, my pictures despise,
My person degrade, and my temper chastise;
And the pen is my terror, the pencil my shame;
All my talents I bury, and dead is my fame.

I am either too low or too highly priz'd;
When elate I am envied, when meek I'm despis'd.

WILLIAM BLAKE
1757 – 1827

Don'ts

Fight your little fight, my boy,
fight and be a man.
Don't be a good little, good little boy
being as good as you can
and agreeing with all the mealy-mouthed, mealy-mouthed
truths that the sly trot out
to protect themselves and their greedy-mouthed, greedy-
    mouthed
cowardice, every old lout.

Don't live up to the dear little girl who costs
you your manhood, and makes you pay.
Nor the dear old mater who so proudly boasts
that you'll make your way.

Don't earn golden opinions, opinions golden,
or at least worth Treasury notes,
from all sorts of men; don't be beholden
to the herd inside the pen.

Don't long to have dear little, dear little boys
whom you'll have to educate
to earn their living; nor yet girls, sweet joys
who will find it so hard to mate.

Nor a dear little home, with its cost, its cost
that you have to pay,
earning your living while your life is lost
and dull death comes in a day.

Don't be sucked in by the su-superior,
don't swallow the culture bait,
don't drink, don't drink and get beerier and beerier,
do learn to discriminate.

Do hold yourself together, and fight
with a hit-hit here and a hit-hit there,
and a comfortable feeling at night
that you've let in a little air.

A little fresh air in the money sty,
knocked a little hole in the holy prison,
done your own little bit, made your own little try
that the risen Christ should be risen.

D. H. LAWRENCE
1885 – 1930

A Man of Words and Not of Deeds

A man of words and not of deeds
Is like a garden full of weeds;
And when the weeds begin to grow,
It's like a garden full of snow;
And when the snow begins to fall,
It's like a bird upon the wall;
And when the bird away does fly,
It's like an eagle in the sky;
And when the sky begins to roar,
It's like a lion at the door;
And when the door begins to crack,
It's like a stick across your back;
And when your back begins to smart,
It's like a penknife in your heart;
And when your heart begins to bleed,
You're dead, and dead, and dead, indeed.

ANON.

Written in Northampton County Asylum

I am! yet what I am who cares, or knows?
   My friends forsake me like a memory lost.
I am the self-consumer of my woes;
   They rise and vanish, an oblivious host,
Shadows of life, whose very soul is lost.
And yet I am – I live – though I am toss'd

Into the nothingness of scorn and noise,
   Into the living sea of waking dream,
Where there is neither sense of life, nor joys,
   But the huge shipwreck of my own esteem
And all that's dear. Even those I loved the best
Are strange – nay, they are stranger than the rest.

I long for scenes where man has never trod –
   For scenes where woman never smiled or wept –
There to abide with my Creator, God,
   And sleep as I in childhood sweetly slept,
Full of high thoughts, unborn. So let me lie, –
The grass below; above, the vaulted sky.

JOHN CLARE
1793 – 1864

A Young Man's Epigram on Existence

A senseless school, where we must give
Our lives that we may learn to live!
A dolt is he who memorizes
Lessons that leave no time for prizes.

THOMAS HARDY
1840 – 1928

When I Have Fears that I May Cease to Be

When I have fears that I may cease to be
Before my pen has glean'd my teeming brain,
Before high-pilèd books, in charact'ry,
Hold like rich garners the full-ripen'd grain;
When I behold, upon the night's starr'd face,
Huge cloudy symbols of a high romance,
And feel that I may never live to trace
Their shadows, with the magic hand of chance;
And when I feel, fair creature of an hour!
That I shall never look upon thee more,
Never have relish in the faery power
Of unreflecting love; – then on the shore
  Of the wide world I stand alone, and think,
  Till Love and Fame to nothingness do sink.

JOHN KEATS
1795 – 1821

Sic Vita

  Like to the falling of a Starre;
  Or as the flights of Eagles are;
  Or like the fresh spring's gawdy hew;
  Or silver drops of morning dew;
  Or like a wind that chafes the flood;
  Or bubbles which on water stood;
  Even such is man, whose borrow'd light
  Is straight call'd in, and paid to night.

* The Wind blowes out; the Bubble dies;*
* The Spring entomb'd in Autumn lies;*
* The Dew dries up; the Starre is shot;*
* The Flight is past; and Man forgot.*

HENRY KING
1592 – 1669

Proportion

It is not growing like a tree
In bulk, doth make man better be;
Or standing long an oak, three hundred year,
To fall a log at last, dry, bald, and sere:
     A lily of a day
     Is fairer far in May,
Although it fall and die that night;
It was the plant and flower of light.
In small proportions we just beauties see;
And in short measures life may perfect be.

BEN JONSON
1573 – 1637

Notes

Some of the contributors and their works

All the poets are in alphabetical order. In the case of the Chinese poets the surname precedes the given name, according to the Chinese custom. For Japanese poets the Western order of names has been followed.

TACHIBANA AKEMI 1812 – 1868   *The Silver Mine*
One of the late traditional *waka* or *tanka* writers of the Tokugawa period in Japan. However, he broke with tradition in his choice of unusual subject-matter. *Tanka* or *waka* are five-line poems composed of 5, 7, 5, 7 and 7 syllables.

CHENG MIN born 1924   *The Ricksha Puller*
A leading woman poet in modern China, Cheng Min was a graduate of the National South-west Associate University in Kunming, where she studied philosophy. She is also a gifted singer, and this can be heard in the tone of her poems, which are elegant and polished. Her work, however, is filled with strong indignation for the inhuman exploitation of her fellow human-beings, as can be seen in this poem.

TSUTOMU FUKUDA born 1905   *The Subway in New York*
One of the best modern Japanese poets writing in English. He is Professor of English language and literature at Tezukayama Women's Junior College, Kobe, and has published several books on English literature and language, including a study of Charles Lamb. His poems in English are published in *Poetry Nippon* and several other Japanese magazines. He is also an expert in *haiku* but prefers free verse when writing in English. *Haiku* is a three-line poem composed of 5, 7 and 5 syllables.

ROBERT GRAVES born 1895   *Warning to Children*
The shape of this poem is interesting: we can think of it as a number of boxes of decreasing size fitted one inside the other. We open box after box until we reach the smallest, then start fitting them together again.

M

HU SHIH 1891 – 1962 *Dream and Poetry*
The acknowledged leader of the Chinese literary revolution, Hu Shih was educated in America. He used daily speech in the writing of poetry in his first volume, *Experiments* (1920), from which this poem is taken. However, he was severely criticized and his work rejected by later Chinese writers.

DENISE LEVERTOV born 1923 *A Map of the Western Part of the County of Essex in England*
This poet, who now lives in America, was born at Ilford in Essex. Those who live in this region will be familiar with the names she uses with such evocative poetic effect. John Betjeman and Stephen Vincent Benét also use proper names in this way.

LOUIS MACNEICE 1907 – 1963 *Prayer before Birth*
This poem is remarkable, not only for the sentiments it expresses, but also for its shape on the printed page. The chromatic indentations and the surging accumulations of the successive verses, rising to 'hands that would spill me' and finishing with the short, dramatic statement 'otherwise kill me', seem to convey vividly both the stages of pregnancy and the various climactic waves in the rhythms of childbirth.

SAPPHO c. 610 B.C. *One Girl*
A Greek woman poet who lived on the island of Lesbos. Her work has been translated by many English poets, among them Lord Byron, D. G. Rossetti, Walter Savage Landor, and by the modern American poet Allen Tate.

TSANG K'O-CHIA born c. 1910 *The Ricksha Puller*
This Chinese poet from Shantung Province adopted the motto of the ancient classical Chinese poet Tu Fu: 'If my words fall short of startling, I won't stop even after death.' He is a most careful craftsman in verse. He had much experience of war and refugees during the Japanese invasion of Manchuria, and much of his poetry, like this poem, is concerned with the plight of suffering humanity. His later poems are much freer in style.

TU FU A.D. 712 – 770 *Overnight in the Apartment by the River*
Tu Fu, noted for his learning, is regarded by the Chinese as their greatest classical poet. Some of his work has been translated by Arthur Waley, but this version of his poem is by William Hung.

WEN I-TO 1899 – 1946   *The Laundry Song*

Born in Hupeh Province, Wen I-To studied Western literature at the only Western-supported college in China, Tsing-hua College. He also had a thorough knowledge of classical Chinese literature, and wrote fine poems in the classical style before changing to the new style using popular speech. He went to America and studied painting at the Art Institute of Chicago and Colorado College. He met famous figures in modern American poetry such as Harriet Monroe, Carl Sandburg and Amy Lowell. But his deepest admiration was for the English Romantic poet John Keats. This poem is the result of his experience in American Chinatowns, and he wrote it, he said, as a Chinese version of Thomas Hood's *The Song of the Shirt* (see page 113). He returned to China in 1925 and after many troubles, literary, domestic and political, he protested against the government in power in the 1930s, the Kuomintang, and against the civil war in China between Nationalists and Communists. He died, the victim of political assassination, on 15th July 1946.

Index of first lines

Like as a huntsman after weary chase, 73
Like the sweet apple which reddens upon the topmost bough, 42
Like to the falling of a Starre, 175
Long time in some forgotten churchyard earth of Warwickshire, 86
Lord of my heart, what have I dreamed, 71
Love bade me welcome: yet my soul drew back, 70

Márgarét, are you gríeving, 16
My father played the melodion, 158
My heart is like a singing bird, 72
My heart leaps up when I behold, 23
My poor old bones – I've only two, 42
My soul is an enchanted boat, 137
My Soul, there is a country, 65
My thoughts hold mortal strife, 81
My true love hath my heart, and I have his, 73

No longer mourn for me when I am dead, 89
Now as I was young and easy under the apple boughs, 27
Now the hungry lion roars, 98

On balmy seas and pernie schooners, 145
Oh would you know why Henry sleeps, 148
(One piece, two pieces, three pieces,), 114
One word is too often profaned, 70
On Linden, when the sun was low, 58
O say! what is that Thing call'd Light, 41
'O what can ail thee, knight-at-arms, 99
O what can you give me, 133
O! why was I born with a different face, 171
O world! O life! O time, 165

Pile the bodies high at Austerlitz and Waterloo, 66
Play it once, 125
Pretty Miss Apathy, 141

Ring out, wild bells, to the wild sky, 161

Shall I compare thee to a Summer's day, 78
she being Brand, 52

Index of authors

Akemi, Tachibana, 48
Anon., 37, 84, 91, 128, 130, 132, 150, 156, 173
Auden, W. H., 50

Bacon, Sir Francis, 166
Barnes, Barnabe, 165
Benét, Stephen Vincent, 24
Betjeman, John, 22, 144
Blake, William, 74, 77, 171
Brontë, Emily, 75
Bullock, Michael (*translator*), 127
Byron, George Gordon, Lord, 53, 169

Campbell, Thomas, 58
Causley, Charles, 33
Cheng Min, 109
Ch'en, Jerome (*translator*), 127
Cibber, Colley, 41
Clare, John, 40, 174
Clough, Arthur Hugh, 147
Coleridge, Samuel Taylor, 101
Cornford, Frances, 83
Cummings, E. E., 52, 146

Davidson, John, 47
Davies, Idris, 133
De la Mare, Walter, 141
Dickinson, Emily, 48, 83, 88
Dimock, E. C. (*translator*), 71
Dixon, Richard Watson, 135
Dowson, Ernest, 82
Drinkwater, John, 86
Drummond, William, of Hawthornden, 81, 153
Dyment, Clifford, 49

Fukuda, Tsutomu, 53

Acknowledgements

Grateful acknowledgements are made to the following for permission to reprint copyright material:

GEORGE ALLEN & UNWIN LTD for 'The Silver Mine' from *An Anthology of Japanese Literature* edited by Donald Keene

ANGUS & ROBERTSON LTD for 'Kite-Flying at Kobe' from *Noonday Country* by Charles Higham

THE ESTATE OF THE LATE S. V. BENÉT and HOLT, RINEHART & WINSTON INC. for 'American Names' from *Selected Poems* by Stephen Vincent Benét, Copyright 1927 by Stephen Vincent Benét, renewed 1955 by Rosemary Carr Benét

JONATHAN CAPE LTD for 'I Wandered' and 'I Remember Arnold' from *In His Own Write* by John Lennon

CHARLES CAUSLEY for his poem 'Guy Fawkes' Day' from *Johnny Alleluia* (Rupert Hart-Davis Ltd)

THE CRESSET PRESS for 'The Watch' from *The Collected Poems of Frances Cornford*

THE LITERARY TRUSTEES OF WALTER DE LA MARE and THE SOCIETY OF AUTHORS as their representatives for 'Pooh' from *The Collected Poems of Walter de la Mare*

J. M. DENT & SONS LTD for an extract from *Gwalia Deserta* by Idris Davies, and 'The Dark City' from *Experiences and Places* by Clifford Dyment; J. M. DENT & SONS LTD and THE TRUSTEES FOR THE COPYRIGHTS OF THE LATE DYLAN THOMAS for 'Fern Hill' from *Collected Poems* by Dylan Thomas

DOUBLEDAY & CO. INC. for 'The Ricksha Puller' by Cheng Min, 'Dream and Poetry' by Hu Shih, 'The Ricksha Puller' by Tsang K'o-chia and 'The Laundry Song' by Wen I-To from *Twentieth Century Chinese Poetry* edited by Kai-Yu Hsu, Copyright © 1963 by Kai-Yu Hsu, and 'From the Bengali' from *In Praise of Krishna* translated by E. C. Dimock and Denise Levertov

GERALD DUCKWORTH & CO. LTD for 'Man Carrying Bale' from *Collected Poems* by Harold Monro

FABER & FABER LTD for 'Night Mail' from *Collected Shorter Poems* by W. H. Auden, 'Prayer before Birth' from *Collected Poems* by Louis MacNeice, 'The River-Merchant's Wife' from *Personae* by Ezra Pound, 'Picture of the Nativity' from *The Stones of Troy* by Constantine Trypanis, and 'The Collier' from *The Ballad of the Mari Lwyd* by Vernon Watkins; FABER & FABER LTD and HARCOURT, BRACE & WORLD INC. for 'she being Brand' from *Poems 1923–1954* by e. e. cummings, Copyright 1926 by Horace Liveright, renewed 1954 by E. E. Cummings, 'anyone lived in a pretty how town' from *Poems*

190